¡BUENOS DÍAS!

The Mexican Breakfast Book

ERICKA SANCHEZ & NICOLE PRESLEY

To my husband, Efrain; my son, Joaquin; my mom, Carmen; and all the *Nibbles and Feasts* readers. —Ericka

I dedicate this book to my Grandfather Sandoval. You were not only my *abuelito*, but you also took the role lovingly as my dad and guiding light, making sure my roots were fully planted deep. *Te quiero con todo mi corazón*, Grandpa! <3 —Nicole

Text and photography copyright © 2023 by Ericka Sanchez and Nicole Presley
All rights reserved.

Published by Familius LLC, www.familius.com
PO Box 1249, Reedley, CA 93654

Familius books are available at special discounts for bulk purchases,
whether for sales promotions or for family or corporate use. For more information, contact
Familius Sales at orders@familius.com.

Reproduction of this book in any manner, in whole or in part,
without written permission of the publisher is prohibited.

Library of Congress Control Number: 2023934748

Print ISBN 9781641709729
EPUB ISBN 9781641709446
Kindle ISBN 9781641709453
Fixed PDF ISBN 9781641709439

Printed in China

Edited by Peg Sandkam and Mikaela Sircable
Cover and book design by Brooke Jorden
Spot photo and cactus pattern sourced from Vecteezy.com

10 9 8 7 6 5 4 3 2 1

First Edition

CONTENTS

Soups ~ Sopas   65

Savory Main ~ Entradas Fuertes   75

Sweet Main ~ Entradas Dulces 138

Sides ~ Guarniciones 163

How to Roast a Poblano Chile

This tried-and-true method can be used in a number of recipes in this book, including the salsa verde [see page 14] and Chiles Rellenos al Horno [see page 76].

1. Rinse poblano chiles and wipe dry with a paper towel. Lightly cover with 1/4 teaspoon oil each. Rub thoroughly and wipe off any excess.

2. Turn stove burner on high. Using tongs, place 1 to 2 poblano chiles on burner, directly over flame.

3. Using metal tongs, turn chiles every 2 to 3 minutes. Allow the skin to blacken on all sides, but do not let the skin turn to ash.

4. Carefully remove the charred chiles with tongs and place them in a clean plastic zip bag. Seal the bag or fold the opening over, leaving some air inside. This will allow the chiles to steam. Steam for at least 10 minutes.

5. Carefully open the zip bag to release hot steam. When the chiles are cool enough to handle, remove them from the bag.

6. Place steamed chiles on a cutting board. Holding the chile by the stem and using the back of a knife or edge of a spoon, scrape the charred skin away from you.

7. Cut each chile in half from the stem to the bottom. Cut off stem and seed cluster; scrape off veins and any extra seeds. Slice in strips and set aside.

Breakfast time has always held a special place in our lives. Whether it's a crowded Sunday morning pozole gathering with our families or an intimate *cafecito con pan* with a close loved one, breakfast is the time of the day where we gain nourishment to be able to meet the day head-on.

As food partners, we have always enjoyed our breakfasts together and carved out *desayuno* as ours. It was during those times when we brainstormed our next project, our next business, our next recipe, or our next trip. Always over a full plate of chilaquiles with an egg (Ericka's extra runny, Nicole's over hard) on top. And it was during one of those breakfasts where we decided to gather our favorite morning recipes and combine them into one special book: *¡Buenos Días!*

From simple salsa to elaborate feasts, you will find something everyone can enjoy in this book. Because of our different backgrounds—Nicole born and raised in the heart of East Los Angeles and Ericka born in Mexico; raised in El Paso, Texas; and now living in Los Angeles—we documented a wide array of breakfast recipes that reflects what we grew up eating on both sides of the border.

El desayuno, breakfast, is considered the most important meal of the day in Mexican and Mexican-American households. It is a time to energize and get ready for the day. It's a time to gather your thoughts.

Start off with fresh fruit, sweet bread, a *jugo* (juice), and coffee as the first course. You then move on to bigger, heartier dishes, usually consisting of eggs, *frijoles*, and corn *masa* in the form of tortillas, tamales, sopes, chilaquiles . . . We can talk forever about breakfast. Even if you're on the go, a *licuado* or burrito will happily make its way out the door with you.

"Never leave the house on an empty stomach."

Many of the recipes in this book are handed down from generation to generation from our immediate and extended families. Others are self-taught from tasting and identifying the right flavors and spices, or from a faded memory of a breakfast calling from years ago.

We hope you enjoy these recipes we have prepared and eaten throughout all aspects of our lives. Some will be authentic Mexican, others will be Mexican with a thin influence of America woven in. But one thing is certain . . . They are going to make your breakfast table a tasty place to start the day.

¡Buenos días!

—Ericka and Nicole

SALSAS

SALSA DE CHILE DE ÁRBOL
Árbol Chile Salsa

Makes 1 1/3 cups
Preparation time: 10 minutes
Cooking time: 10 minutes

This chile de árbol salsa is perfectly spicy. A bit goes a long way because it can really pack a punch! Ideal for giving scrambled eggs a kick or to turn your white chicken pozole [see page 73] red and spicy.
—Ericka

1/4 cup vegetable oil

3/4 cup dried árbol chiles, stems removed

1 cup water, divided

2 cloves of garlic

1/2 teaspoon salt

1. Heat oil in a medium skillet over medium heat. Add árbol chiles and stir. Lightly fry for 2 minutes, stirring rapidly. Do not burn.

2. Reduce heat to low and add 3/4 cup water to cover chiles. Simmer for 5 minutes.

3. Transfer chiles and liquid to a blender; add garlic and salt. Blend until smooth. Add additional water a teaspoon at a time if salsa is too thick.

4. Transfer to a serving bowl and serve.

SALSA DE JARDÍN
Garden Salsa

Makes 4 cups
Preparation time: 5 minutes
Cooking time: 35 minutes

This is an everyday salsa that is made of fresh chiles and tomatoes. The addition of chopped cilantro and green onion to the salsa brings a welcomed texture and freshness. Salsa de jardín *can be enjoyed in a breakfast burrito or drizzled over eggs. It keeps for up to a week in the fridge.* —Nicole

1/2 tablespoon vegetable oil
1/2 large white onion, cut in quarters
3 cloves of garlic
2 tablespoons + 2 teaspoons salt, divided
4 Roma tomatoes
1 dried árbol chile

2 serrano chiles
3 jalapeño chiles
3 yellow chiles
5 stalks green onion
1/3 cup cilantro leaves
1 1/2 teaspoons black pepper

1. Heat vegetable oil in a frying pan over medium heat.

2. Sauté white onion and garlic in oil until browned. Remove from pan and set aside.

3. Fill one large pot halfway with water. Bring water to a boil over medium-high heat. Add 2 table-spoons of salt, tomatoes, árbol chile, serrano chiles, jalapeños, and yellow chiles. Allow to boil for 25 to 35 minutes or until tomatoes and chiles can be easily pierced with a fork.

4. Remove and dispose of the árbol chile stem. Reserve 2 cups of water and drain the rest.

5. Cut off and discard the green portion of the green onion; slice the remaining white portion extremely thin. Coarsely chop cilantro leaves. Set aside green onion and cilantro.

6. Add 1 cup reserved water and sautéed onion and garlic to a blender along with the boiled tomatoes and árbol chile. Blend until smooth.

7. Pour into a large mixing bowl.

8. Add 2 teaspoons salt, remaining chiles, pepper, and remaining reserved water to the blender. Blend until smooth.

9. Pour over tomato mixture in the bowl.

10. Mix sliced green onion and chopped cilantro into the salsa with a large spoon.

   Tip for extra salsa: You can either divide your salsa up into small jars and share with friends or freeze the salsa in ice cubes and use when cooking something that needs an extra burst of flavor, like a soup or chopped meat.

SALSA VERDE
Green Salsa

Makes 3 cups
Preparation time: 10 minutes
Cooking time: 35 minutes

This versatile salsa verde *can be transformed into just about anything.* **Chicharrón en salsa verde** *[see page 123] ,* **huevos divorciados** *[see page 99] , and* **chilaquiles verdes con chicharrón** *[see page 112] are just a few uses for this sauce. It's also a great salsa to enjoy with chips. Make plenty and freeze in batches to enjoy when needed!* —Ericka

8 cups water

2 jalapeño chiles

3 serrano chiles

1 3/4 pounds tomatillo, husked and rinsed

2 poblano chiles

1/4 cup vegetable oil, divided

1/2 cup white onion, roughly chopped

3 cloves of garlic

2/3 cup fresh cilantro, roughly chopped

1 1/4 cups chicken broth (or water), divided

1/2 teaspoon salt

1. Bring water to a boil over medium heat. Add jalapeños and serranos. Boil for 5 minutes.

2. Add tomatillos and continue boiling for 8 minutes or until tomatillos darken. Turn off heat and let them cool in water before draining.

3. Remove stems from the boiled chiles.

4. Roast poblanos over an open flame until char spots evenly form on all sides. [See detailed instructions on page 5.] Transfer to a clean plastic zip bag, seal, and let steam for 10 minutes.

5. Carefully remove poblanos from bag. Scrape charred skin off with a spoon or the back of a knife. Remove and dispose of seeds and stem. Set aside poblanos.

6. Heat 2 tablespoons oil in a large skillet over medium heat. Lightly fry onion and garlic, about 2 minutes. Transfer to blender.

7. Add boiled chiles, tomatillos, poblanos, cilantro, and 1/2 cup of chicken broth. Pulse a few times until desired consistency.

8. Heat remaining oil in skillet over medium heat. Add blended mixture, remaining broth, and salt; simmer for 12 minutes. Adjust salt if needed.

    Note: This salsa can be enjoyed hot or cold!

CURTIDO DE JALAPEÑO, SERRANO Y CEBOLLA

Pickled Jalapeño, Serrano, and Onions

Makes 1 3/4 cups
Preparation time: 15 minutes
Refrigeration time: 1 hour

You don't need a stove, blender, or molcajete *to make this spicy morning accompaniment. All you need is a good knife and chopping board to slice a few ingredients. Serve these pickled veggies with your morning eggs or on top of your favorite chilaquiles.* —Ericka

3/4 cup white onion, thinly sliced

2 large jalapeño chiles, thinly sliced

2 large serrano chiles, thinly sliced

1/3 cup lime juice

1/3 cup olive oil

1/2 teaspoon salt

1. Combine all ingredients in a large bowl. Toss with a fork to mix well.

2. Refrigerate for 1 hour before serving.

SALSA ASADA
Spicy Roasted Salsa

Makes 2 cups
Preparation time: 5 minutes
Cooking time: 30 minutes

I call this one the "hangover salsa." It's the best cure after a night of celebrating. The spiciness is mellow and tolerable. Perfect with tortilla chips and as a sauce for your huevos rancheros *[see page 127].*
—Ericka

7 Roma tomatoes

1 jalapeño chile

3 serrano chiles

1/3 cup white onion, roughly chopped

2 cloves of garlic, roughly chopped

1/3 cup water

1 tablespoon cooking oil

1/2 teaspoon sea salt

1. Heat skillet or *comal* over high heat. Place tomatoes, jalapeño, and serranos on skillet and roast, turning frequently, until charred spots form on all sides. Remove from heat and let cool.

2. Cut off and dispose of chile stems and tomato stem scars. Roughly chop remaining chiles and tomatoes; transfer to a blender.

3. Add onion, garlic, and water. Pulse until salsa is blended with texture.

4. Heat oil in a medium saucepan over medium heat. Carefully pour in salsa, add salt, and cook for 15 minutes. Remove from heat and serve.

SALSA DE CHILE GÜERO
Yellow Chile Salsa

Makes 2 cups
Preparation time: 10 minutes
Cooking time: 20 minutes

Salsa de chile güero *is one of the most flavorful salsas with a hint of heat. Triangular-shaped, blonde-yellow* chile güero *is a mild-flavored chile and is the main ingredient in this salsa. It works well poured on eggs, as a chile base to* chilaquiles güeros *[see page 136], or served in a breakfast taco.* —Nicole

1 teaspoon vegetable oil

1/2 medium white onion, chopped

6 cloves of garlic, smashed

8 yellow chiles

3 large tomatillos, husked and rinsed

1 serrano chile

1 1/2 teaspoons olive oil

1 1/2 teaspoons sea salt

1 tablespoon avocado

1/4 cup hot water

1/2 teaspoon pepper

1. Brush a griddle or *comal* with vegetable oil and place over a medium-high heat until cooking surface is hot.

2. Place onion, garlic, yellow chiles, tomatillos, and serrano chile on the cooking surface. Everything will roast/cook at different times. Keep an eye on ingredients and remove from *comal*/griddle after they char on all sides. The garlic will be the first to brown (this will take 3 to 5 minutes), while the yellow chile and serrano chile will take the most time (around 20 minutes). Move ingredients around to ensure even roasting.

3. Once roasted, remove stems from yellow chiles and serrano chile.

   For a chunky salsa (pictured), I recommend grinding with a large *molcajete y tejolote* (mortar and pestle).

4. Add olive oil, sea salt, garlic, and avocado to the *molcajete*, then grind into a pureed paste.

5. Add hot water and pieces of roasted onion. Grind onion a little at a time into the garlic-avocado puree.

6. Grind in one tomatillo at a time. If you puncture the tomatillo once, it will keep the tomatillo from splattering and will be easier to grind.

7. Lastly add the chiles. Adding them one at a time makes it easier to grind into the salsa.

8. Sprinkle with pepper and mix.

   For a smooth salsa: Add roasted ingredients to blender and top with olive oil, sea salt, avocado, hot water, and pepper. Pulse until all ingredients come together and the salsa is smooth.

DRINKS

Bebidas

ATOLE DE AMARANTO

Amaranth Atole

Serves 6
Preparation time: 10 minutes
Cooking time: 30 minutes

Amaranth atole has a delicious, nutty flavor that is comforting and soothing. Enjoy it on a cold winter morning with a slice of buttered toast. It doesn't get any better than that! —Ericka

2 cups puffed amaranth, plus more for garnish

2 tablespoons cornstarch

1/2 cup water, warm

6 cups whole milk, divided

1 cinnamon stick

1/2 cup sugar

1/4 teaspoon salt

1 teaspoon vanilla extract

1. Place amaranth in a medium skillet over low heat. Stir until amaranth is fragrant and toasted, about 3 minutes. Do not burn. Immediately remove from heat and transfer to a blender.

2. Whisk together cornstarch and water in a small bowl. Set aside.

3. Place 4 cups milk and cinnamon stick in a large saucepan over medium-low heat. Bring to a low simmer.

4. Add the remaining milk to amaranth in blender. Blend until smooth. Set aside.

5. Add sugar, salt, and vanilla to simmering milk. Stir until sugar dissolves, about 5 minutes.

6. Discard cinnamon stick and add blended amaranth mixture and cornstarch mixture. Stir constantly until mixture thickens, about 15 minutes.

7. Garnish with a sprinkle of puffed amaranth and serve.

LICUADO DE PLÁTANO Y ALMENDRA

Banana Almond Smoothie

Serves 2
Preparation time: 5 minutes

Licuados *are the fastest way to enjoy a nutritious breakfast on the run. This smoothie is a combination of milk and banana with little crunchy bits of almond. Use frozen bananas in the summer months for an extra cold, slushy drink.* —Nicole

20 raw almonds

2 ripe bananas, fresh or frozen

2 tablespoons honey

3 cups milk or oat milk

1/2 teaspoon vanilla

1/8 teaspoon ground cinnamon

1. Add almonds, bananas, honey, milk, and vanilla to a blender. Blend for 2 minutes.

2. Pour evenly into serving cups and sprinkle with cinnamon.

CÓCTEL DE GUAYABA Y CHAMPÁN CON FRESAS

Boozy Guava Strawberry Champagne

Serves 2
Preparation time: 5 minutes

What's Sunday brunch without a champagne cocktail? This lovely little sparkler is sure to liven up your desayuno. *The combo of fresh strawberries, guava nectar, and a splash of champagne is everything I dream of on a Sunday morning.* —Nicole

2 strawberries

2 tablespoons lime juice, divided

1/2 cup guava nectar, divided

1/2 cup champagne, divided

1. Remove and discard strawberry stems. Chop strawberries into small cubes and divide among two champagne flutes.
2. Add 1 tablespoon lime juice over strawberries in each flute.
3. Pour 1/4 cup guava nectar over strawberries in each flute.
4. Top with 1/4 cup champagne in each flute.

PONCHE DE FRUTAS

Breakfast Fruit Punch

Serves 8
Preparation time: 15 minutes

This breakfast drink can be enjoyed on its own as a morning boost or as an accompaniment to a meal. It can be modified with fresh or canned fruit depending on the season. It's perfect year-round and even makes a great frozen pop for summer snacking. —Ericka

2 large Fuji apples, cored, peeled, and chopped

8 slices canned yellow peaches in heavy syrup

1/2 cup syrup from canned peaches

1/2 cup lime juice

2 oranges, seeds removed, peeled, and as much of the pith removed as possible

1 cup canned pineapple chunks in pineapple juice

1/2 cup canned pineapple juice from pineapple chunks

1/3 cup grenadine syrup (optional)

3 cups water

Mint sprigs for garnish

1. Place all ingredients except water and mint in blender. Blend until smooth; approximately 45 seconds.

2. Stir in water.

3. Pour in serving glasses and garnish with mint.

AGUA DE NOPAL Y TOMATILLO
Cactus and Tomatillo Cooler

Serves 6
Preparation time: 10 minutes

This vigorous morning refresher will help you start the day. Abundant in antioxidants, vitamin C, and electrolytes, this is the perfect beverage to help you get the day started. —Ericka

2 cactus pads

8 cups water

1/2 cup granulated sugar

1 tomatillo, husked and chopped

1/2 cup lime juice

Ice (optional)

1. Scrape off and dispose of the thorns from the cactus pads.

2. Rinse and chop the cactus.

3. Combine water and sugar in a large pitcher. Stir to dissolve sugar.

4. Place cactus, tomatillo, lime juice, and 1 cup sweetened water from the pitcher in a blender. Blend until smooth.

5. Add blended mixture to pitcher. Stir to mix well.

6. Serve with or without ice.

HORCHATA CREMOSA
Creamy Horchata

Makes 12 cups
Preparation time: 25 minutes
Resting time: 10 hours or overnight

Sometimes we just need a nice agua de horchata *to start our day as the weather goes from warm to hot. Horchata is an excellent drink to serve with a spicy breakfast, as its creamy components help balance the spice.* —Nicole

5 cups + 5 cups cold water, divided

2 Mexican cinnamon sticks

2 cups long grain rice

1/2 cup almonds

2 1/2 teaspoons vanilla extract

1 1/2 cups sugar

1 1/2 cups heavy cream or whole milk

Ground cinnamon for serving (optional)

1. Bring 5 cups of water and cinnamon sticks to a boil in a pot over medium-high heat.

2. Place rice and almonds in a heat-proof bowl and pour the boiling water and cinnamon sticks over rice. Cover bowl with plastic wrap and allow to steep and soak for 10 hours.

3. Remove 1 cinnamon stick.

4. Blend mixture on high until cinnamon and rice are completely blended.

5. Strain blended mixture through a cheesecloth-lined sieve into a large pitcher. Discard cheesecloth and any rice/almond paste collected in sieve.

6. Rinse blender clean to remove any rice remnants. Add vanilla, 5 cups cold water, and sugar to blender and blend on high until sugar is dissolved.

7. Pour sugar water into rice/cinnamon water, then pour in milk and stir to combine completely.

8. Chill in fridge until cold.

9. Serve cold over ice and topped with ground cinnamon.

CAFÉ HELADO DE HORCHATA
Creamy Horchata Iced Coffee

Makes 4 cups
Preparation time: 30 minutes
Cooling time: 30 minutes

This horchata pick-me-up is perfect for the summer months when the heat greets you first thing in the morning. Swap out creamer for sweetened horchata instead. It adds the perfect amount of creaminess to the coffee and leaves you with an extra bounce in your step. —Nicole

2 1/2 cups water

6 tablespoons coffee grounds, medium roast

1/4 cup piloncillo or brown sugar, packed (optional)

4 cups ice

2 cups creamy horchata [see page 35]

1. Bring water to a boil in a small pot over medium-high heat.

2. Add coffee grounds and piloncillo or brown sugar to water and mix to combine. Continue boiling for 5 minutes or until piloncillo is dissolved.

3. Remove from heat and allow to steep for 10 minutes.

4. Strain coffee through cheesecloth-lined sieve to collect all coffee grounds. Allow coffee mixture to come to room temperature, around 30 minutes.

5. Fill four cups with ice. Pour 1/2 cup coffee over ice into each cup. Then slowly pour in 1/2 cup horchata over coffee and ice.

   Tip: If you don't enjoy sweet coffee, omit the sugar. If you desire more sugar, add another 1/4 cup.

TÉ DE YERBA BUENA Y MIEL
Honey Mint Tea

Makes 2–3 cups
Preparation time: 10 minutes
Steeping time: 10 minutes

Comforting yerba buena *tea slightly sweetened with honey gently helps start the day. This tea is reserved for mornings when lounging is encouraged and self-care is priority.* —Nicole

3 cups water
3 sprigs mint

3 tablespoons honey

1. Pour water in a small pot over medium-high heat.
2. Bring water to a boil, then remove from heat.
3. Add mint to water and allow to steep for 10 minutes.
4. Drizzle in honey and stir to combine.
5. Serve in two or three cups. Enjoy warm.

BATIDO DE MANGO Y AVENA

Mango Oat Smoothie

Serves 2
Preparation time: 10 minutes

No time for breakfast? Prep this smoothie the night before. Blend in the morning and go! This vita-min-loaded smoothie will keep you full until lunchtime. Use ripe mangoes for a sweeter drink. —Ericka

1 1/2 cups mango pulp

1 cup + 2 teaspoons rolled oats, divided

2 tablespoons honey

1 1/2 cups milk of your choice

1 1/2 cups ice

Blueberries for serving

Mint sprigs for serving

1. Place mango, 1 cup oats, honey, milk, and ice in blender. Blend until smooth.

2. Divide mixture between two serving glasses and top with remaining oats, blueberries, and mint.

CAFÉ DE OLLA
Mexican Spiced Coffee

Makes 6 cups
Preparation time: 5 minutes
Cooking time: 15 minutes
Steeping time: 10 minutes

This delicious, sweet, Mexican cinnamon–spiced coffee is enjoyed starting first thing in the morning. This is typically made in a clay pot (olla de barro), which gives the coffee its signature flavor, and is sweetened with piloncillo, an unrefined cone-shaped sugar that tastes similar to molasses. Café de olla, an ideal way to warm up at the beginning of a cold day. —Nicole

6 cups water

6 ounces piloncillo

1 Mexican cinnamon stick

1 tablespoon vanilla

1 clove

6 tablespoons coffee grounds, medium roast

1.   Bring water, piloncillo, cinnamon stick, vanilla, and clove to a boil in a clay or enamel pot over medium-high heat. It should take about 15 minutes for the water to boil and the piloncillo to dissolve. Remove from heat.

2.   Pour coffee grounds into liquid and mix to combine. Allow coffee to steep for 10 minutes.

3.   Strain liquid through a cheesecloth-lined sieve into cups or a different pot. Serve hot and enjoy.

ATOLE DE AVENA

Oat Atole

Serves 6
Preparation time: 5 minutes
Cooking time: 15 minutes

Oat atole is our go-to during those frigid winter mornings. It is a comforting drink that pairs perfectly with red prickly pear tostadas [see page 217] and makes you feel warm and cozy. It's perfect to dunk your pan dulce in too. —Ericka

2 1/4 cups water

1 cinnamon stick

1 can (12 ounces) evaporated milk

2 1/2 cups milk

1 teaspoon vanilla extract

1/2 cup whole oats

1/2 cup sugar

1. Combine water and cinnamon stick in a large saucepan over medium heat. Bring to a boil.

2. Reduce heat to a simmer and cover.

3. In a blender, combine milks, vanilla, and oats. Blend until smooth.

4. Add sugar to water and cinnamon; stir to dissolve completely.

5. Add milk mixture and stir frequently for 15 minutes or until liquid thickens. Serve immediately.

NARANJADA

Orangeade

Serves 4
Preparation time: 10 minutes
Chilling time: 2 hours

I welcome all bubbly drinks, and this refreshing sparkling orange juice happens to be one of my favorite breakfast beverages! It's a nice way to get your vitamin C and quench your thirst at the same time. I like to think of it as a natural soda, fizzy and sweet. —Nicole

8 oranges, divided

2 large limes, divided

1/4 cup sugar

2 cups mineral water

Ice

1. Rinse 7 oranges and 1 lime under cold water.

2. Cut citrus in half and juice until all liquid is extracted and collected in a bowl. Remove any seeds that fall into juice.

3. Mix juice and sugar together in a pitcher until sugar is dissolved.

4. Place in the refrigerator to chill for 2 hours.

5. Add mineral water to pitcher and mix.

6. Divide ice among four glasses.

7. Pour *naranjada* over ice.

8. Garnish with orange and lime slices from the remaining fruit.

AGUA FRESCA DE TUNA ROJA Y PIÑA

Prickly Pear and Pineapple Cooler

Serves 6
Preparation time: 15 minutes

Start your mornings with nutrient-rich prickly pear and pineapples. This agua fresca *is not only refreshing but so good for you. Want to omit sugar? Select prickly pears and a pineapple at their peak ripeness. Their natural sweetness will be enough to either omit the sugar quantity in this recipe or decrease it.*
—Ericka

8 medium red prickly pears, peeled and roughly chopped

2 cups pineapple, roughly chopped

8 cups water, divided

1/2 cup sugar

1 tablespoon lime juice

Ice (optional)

1. Combine prickly pears, pineapple, and 1 cup water in a blender. Blend until smooth.

2. Place remaining water, sugar, and lime juice in a large pitcher. Stir until sugar has dissolved.

3. Strain prickly pear and pineapple mixture into pitcher. Stir to combine.

4. Serve with or without ice.

LECHE DE FRESA
Strawberry Milk

Serves 2
Preparation time: 5 minutes
Cooking time: 10 minutes

Strawberry milk is a quick, fun, and easy drink for kids and adults. This beverage can be made with any type of milk, whole or plant-based. One thing is for sure: the strawberries must be nice and ripe to get the best, most intense flavor. —Ericka

1 3/4 cups diced fresh strawberries

2 tablespoons granulated sugar

1 tablespoon lime juice

2 tablespoons water

2 cups milk, divided

1. Combine strawberries, sugar, lime juice, and water in a medium saucepan over medium heat. Boil for 10 minutes and stir frequently until strawberries begin to fall apart and mixture is thick enough to coat the back of a metal spoon.

2. Remove from heat and let cool completely.

3. Divide strawberry mixture between two serving glasses.

4. Add milk to each glass, stir, and enjoy.

SALADS

Ensaladas

BIONICO

Bionic Breakfast Salad

Serves 4
Preparation time: 20 minutes

This fruity salad is named "bionic" in Spanish because it's the epitome of what you might eat if you wanted to be super strong. It's a great way to use up the last of the fruits you have on hand. The fruits used in this salad can be exchanged for any fruit you love and want to add—no fruit addition is off-limits! —Nicole

1 1/2 cups red grapes, sliced in quarters

2 bananas, sliced

1 1/2 cups mango, chopped

1 1/2 cups melon, cubed

1 cup blueberries

1 cup orange, cubed

1 cup cherries, pitted

2 tablespoons sugar

1/2 cup crema mexicana

1/2 cup vanilla yogurt

1/4 cup raisins, divided

1/4 cup shredded sweetened coconut, divided

1/2 cup granola, divided

1. Mix all fruit together in a bowl.

2. Divide the fruit into four serving bowls/cups.

3. In a separate bowl, combine sugar, crema mexicana, and yogurt.

4. Pour 1/4 cup cream mixture over each cup of fruit.

5. Top each cup with 1 tablespoon of raisins and 1 tablespoon of coconut, then sprinkle 2 tablespoons of granola over each cup.

ENSALADA DE NOPAL CURADO

Cured Cactus Salad

Serves 6
Preparation time: 15 minutes

This refreshing salad is one of the quickest salads I've ever prepared. My favorite is seeing the foamy gel form when massaging the cactus strips; they immediately transform into soft noodle-like green strips. You will love this as a side salad or as a topping to black bean and corn soup [see page 66]. —Ericka

1 1/2 pounds cactus pads

1/2 cup salt

1/2 cup red onion, sliced

2 Roma tomatoes, finely chopped

1–2 habanero chiles, thinly sliced

1/4 cup fresh cilantro, chopped

1/4 teaspoon black pepper

1 tablespoon lime juice

1. Scrape off and dispose of the thorns from the cactus pads.

2. Rinse and slice cactus lengthwise into thin strips.

3. Place strips in a large bowl and add salt. Toss for 10 minutes with hands until strips soften and a gelatinous foam forms. It will resemble dish soap.

4. Transfer strips to a colander and rinse until all foam and gel drains.

5. Move strips to a large salad bowl. Add onion, tomatoes, habanero chiles, cilantro, pepper, and lime juice. Toss to combine ingredients. Serve immediately.

ENSALADA DE QUESO FRESCO, SERRANO Y TOMATE

Fresh Cheese Serrano Tomato Salad

Serves 4
Preparation time: 10 minutes

A simple and flavorful addition to the plate. This salad is best enjoyed during the summer months when the heat is unbearable and tomatoes are at the peak of their season. Enjoy with a side of hard-boiled eggs or a crusty bolillo. —Nicole

4 small tomatoes

1/2 teaspoon salt

1/4 teaspoon pepper

1 serrano chile, sliced into rounds

1/2 small red onion, sliced

3 tablespoons olive oil

1 tablespoon orange juice

1 tablespoon lime juice

1 clove of garlic, finely minced

Pinch of oregano

1/4 cup cilantro

1 cup queso fresco, crumbled in chunks

1. Cut tomatoes into wedges and toss with salt and pepper. Set aside.

2. Toss serrano chile rounds and red onion over tomato wedges.

3. In a separate bowl, whisk together olive oil, orange juice, lime juice, garlic, and oregano.

4. Pour dressing over tomatoes.

5. Sprinkle in cilantro leaves and queso fresco.

ENSALADA DE PANELA, SANDIA, DURAZNO Y PEPINO

Marinated Panela Cheese with Watermelon, Peach, and Cucumber Salad

Serves 6
Preparation time: 10 minutes
Refrigeration time: 30 minutes

This is the best salad in the summertime to wake up to! The complementing flavors of fresh chunks of watermelon, sweet peaches, and cool cucumbers come together with mint and marinated panela cheese. Save time and prepare the marinated cheese the night before. —Ericka

1 package (10 ounces) panela cheese, cubed

1/4 cup white wine vinegar

3 tablespoons extra virgin olive oil

1 teaspoon dried crushed oregano

1/2 teaspoon salt

2 cups cubed watermelon

2 cups cubed peaches

1 cup cubed cucumber

1/2 cup fresh mint, chopped

1 lime, juiced

1. Combine cheese, vinegar, oil, oregano, and salt in a medium bowl. Toss to combine.

2. Refrigerate for 30 minutes to overnight.

3. In a large bowl, combine watermelon, peaches, cucumber, and mint. Add marinated cheese and lime juice. Toss to combine.

ENSALADA XE'EC

Xe'ec Salad

Serves 4
Preparation time: 15 minutes

Pronounced "check," meaning "mixture" (or "revoltijo" in Mayan), this Yucatecan salad is tangy, sweet, spicy, loaded with vitamin C, and the perfect way to start off the day. This salad is traditionally served for the Hanal Pixán *holiday, the day of the dead celebration in Yucatan.* Hanal *means "food" and* pixán *means "soul that gives life to the body." A great accompaniment to hardy, high-fat meals, such as fried eggs or tamales.* —Ericka

3 navel oranges, divided

1 1/2 cups julienned jicama

2 tablespoons lime juice

1 large grapefruit

2 mandarins

1/4 cup fresh cilantro, finely chopped

1/2 teaspoon sea salt

2 tablespoons dried pequín chiles, crushed

1. Juice 1 orange.

2. Combine jicama, lime juice, and orange juice in a large bowl; stir to coat well and set aside.

3. Peel grapefruit, mandarins, and remaining oranges and separate wedges.

4. Using a small knife, remove as much of the pith as possible and chop into bite-sized pieces.

5. Add to bowl with jicama and juices.

6. Add cilantro, salt, and pequín chiles. Toss to mix well and serve.

SOUPS
Sopas

CALDO DE FRIJOL NEGRO Y MAÍZ

Black Bean and Corn Soup

Serves 8
Preparation time: 10 minutes
Cooking time: 2 hours 5 minutes

A black bean soup really hits the spot on cold mornings. I love making this black bean and corn soup for Sunday brunch because it reminds me of a meatless pozole. It's also great for a hangover cure! To take it to the next level, top it with cured cactus salad [see page 57]. —Ericka

SOUP

1 1/2 cups dried black beans, rinsed and debris removed

10 cups water, divided

3 cups fresh white corn kernels, rinsed and debris removed

3 cloves of garlic

1/4 large onion

2 teaspoons salt

Epazote sprig (with about 12 leaves)

GARNISH

Chopped onion

Red chile flakes

Chopped jalapeño chile

Crushed dried oregano

Lime juice

Corn tortillas, warmed

1. Combine beans and 4 cups water in a large saucepan over medium heat. Bring to a boil for 5 minutes, then reduce heat to medium-low. Cook for 45 minutes.

2. Add remaining water, corn, garlic, onion, salt, and epazote. Cook on medium-low for 1 hour and 15 minutes or until beans are tender. Adjust salt if necessary.

3. Serve with chopped onion, red chile flakes, jalapeños, oregano, lime juice, and tortillas.

MENUDO
Spicy Hominy and Tripe Soup

Serves 10
Preparation time: 1 hour 30 minutes
Cooking time: 5 hours

Sunday morning is reserved for a bowl of hot menudo. *It is a traditional meal shared by many Mexican families* el domingo. *It is also known as* pancita, *which translates to "little stomach," as the base of the soup is made with tripe (the lining of the cow's stomach). It is one of the most delicious soups with a hearty red chile broth, meaty tripe, and hominy. While my family dunks fresh bolillos into the broth and eats the bread alongside the bowl of* menudo, *many people opt for a tortilla instead. Either way is excellent! This soup is a labor of love and takes many hours to make. I suggest making it on Saturday to be enjoyed Sunday morning. Leftovers can be frozen in an airtight container for up to three months. —Nicole*

SOUP

4 pounds tripe

4 pounds honeycomb tripe

Hot water, enough to fill half a basin

3 tablespoons white vinegar

3 tablespoons fresh lemon juice

1 white onion

10 cloves of garlic, divided

1 bay leaf

2 ounces dried guajillo chile

3 ounces dried New Mexico chile

3 ounces dried California chile

1 ounce árbol chile

1 large dried pasilla chile

1/2 teaspoon ground cumin

3 tablespoons salt

1 can (110 ounces) Mexican-style hominy, drained

GARNISH

Chopped onion

Fresh cilantro

Dried oregano

Red chile flakes

Lemon, cut in quarters

1. Soak tripe and honeycomb tripe in a large basin covered with hot water, vinegar, and lemon juice for 1 hour to ensure the meat is clean.

2. Drain and rinse all tripe. If the tripe is not cut already, cut into 2-inch cubes.

3. Place tripe, onion, 5 garlic cloves, and bay leaf in a large pot covered by 3 inches of water over medium-high heat. Bring water to a boil.

4. Cover pot with a lid and reduce to a simmer for 3 hours.

5. While tripe is simmering, in a separate pot, boil guajillo chile, New Mexico chile, California chile, árbol chile, and pasilla chile for 30 minutes or until dried chiles are softened.

6. Reserve 1 cup of water; drain the rest.

7. Remove stems from all chiles and place in a blender, along with reserved chile water, remaining garlic cloves, cumin, and salt. Blend until smooth, about 3 minutes.

8. Pour blended chile mixture through a sieve (to collect any remaining seeds and chile skin) into a medium bowl. Scrape sieve with a spoon to help chile pass through. Set aside.

9. After tripe has simmered for 3 hours, remove the lid and skim the fat layer off the top of the broth with a spoon.

10. Replenish the tripe soup with a few cups of water to retain the 3 inches of water above the tripe.

11. Add strained chile and hominy to tripe mixture. Mix to combine and simmer for another 2 hours.

12. Once *menudo* is fully cooked, skim the top one last time to remove any fat from broth. Discard onion and bay leaf.

13. Serve hot garnished with chopped onion, cilantro, oregano, red chile flakes, and a squeeze of lemon juice.

14. Eat with fresh bolillos or corn tortillas.

Tip: When purchasing the tripe, ask the butcher to clean and cut the tripe into 2-inch pieces/cubes for you.

Note: Many people add the pig foot (*pata*) to the boiling process of the tripe. It is believed to give the broth a richer flavor. This is an optional step. If you desire to use the pig foot, I recommend buying a 1 1/2–pound pig foot/leg from the butcher when purchasing the tripe. You will add the pig foot into the pot when you begin to boil the tripe. It carries the same cooking time.

POZOLE BLANCO DE POLLO

White Chicken Pozole

Serves 8
Preparation time: 20 minutes
Cooking time: 2 hours 5 minutes

White pozole makes a great breakfast dish for the entire family. The spicy salsa, whether red or green, is added after serving. Children and adults who don't eat spicy food can omit the salsa and enjoy it as is. This chicken pozole can be topped with lettuce or cabbage, radishes, avocado, and lots of lime juice.
—Ericka

SOUP

2 1/2 cups canned hominy, rinsed thoroughly

8 cups + 1/3 cup water, divided

1/2 large white onion, roughly chopped

4 cloves of garlic

1 teaspoon dried oregano

3 pounds chicken thighs, with bone and skin

4 cups chicken broth

1 teaspoon salt, or to taste

Tostadas to serve

GARNISH

Shredded lettuce

Sliced radishes

Sliced avocado

Chopped onion

Dried crushed oregano

Fresh lime juice

Árbol chile salsa [see page 10]

1. Combine hominy with 8 cups water in a large stock pot over medium heat. Boil for 90 minutes or until hominy is tender.

2. Combine onion, garlic, oregano, and 1/3 cup water in a blender. Blend until smooth.

3. Add blended onion mixture to boiled hominy. Add chicken and chicken broth. When the liquid comes back to a boil, remove and discard the layer of foam that rises to the top.

4. Add salt and continue boiling for another 35 minutes or until chicken has cooked.

5. Remove chicken from pot and place in a large bowl. Let the pieces cool to the touch.

6. Remove and discard the skin and bones from the chicken pieces. Shred the chicken meat with fingers and return to the pot.

7. Ladle pozole into serving bowls. Top with lettuce, radishes, avocado, onion, oregano, lime juice, and árbol chile salsa.

SAVORY MAIN

Entradas Fuertes

CHILES RELLENOS AL HORNO PARA DESAYUNAR

Baked Breakfast Stuffed Chiles

Serves 4
Preparation time: 30 minutes
Baking time: 50 minutes
Cooling time: 10 minutes

Many hours are poured into making chiles rellenos, *which take a good percentage of the day to prepare. This baked version eliminates a few steps out of the process, is equally delicious, and can serve a small group of people for a Sunday brunch.* —Nicole

4 poblano chiles or Anaheim chiles	1/2 teaspoon salt
1 cup queso fresco, crumbled	1/2 teaspoon pepper
5 eggs, divided yolk from whites	1 cup grated Oaxaca cheese
1/2 cup milk	Crema mexicana for serving
2 tablespoons flour	Garden salsa [see page 13], for serving

1. Preheat oven to 350°F.

2. Roast chiles on an open flame until completely charred. [See detailed instructions on page 5.]

3. Place roasted chiles in an airtight bag for 20 minutes and allow to steam in their own heat.

4. Scrape charred skin off with a butter knife until skin is smooth.

5. Make a slit in the chiles and stuff each with 1/4 cup queso fresco. Set aside.

6. Grease a 9x9 baking dish.

7. In a large mixing bowl, whisk egg yolks, milk, flour, salt, and pepper. Set aside.

8. Whisk egg whites in a stand mixer until peaks form.

9. Gently fold egg whites into egg yolk mixture.

10. Pour half of egg mixture into baking dish.

11. Place stuffed chiles over eggs, then pour the remaining egg mixture over chiles.

12. Sprinkle the top with Oaxaca cheese.

13. Bake on middle rack for 30 minutes. The top should be a nice golden brown.

14. Remove from oven and cover with a piece of aluminum foil. Place back in the oven and continue baking for an additional 20 minutes.

15. Remove from oven and allow to cool for 10 minutes before serving.

16. Top with crema mexicana and garden salsa.

HUEVO Y PAPAS CON CHORIZO AL HORNO
Baked Egg, Potato, and Chorizo Casserole

Serves 4
Preparation time: 10 minutes
Cooking time: 1 hour

Make this easy casserole next time you have guests over for breakfast or brunch. The layered shredded potato, baked eggs, spicy roasted salsa, and chorizo make this a complete flavorful meal. It's perfect wrapped up in warm flour tortillas or scooped up with crispy corn chips. —Ericka

2 1/2 cups shredded Yukon Gold potato

1/3 cup sliced white onion

2 teaspoons olive oil

1/2 teaspoon salt

1/4 teaspoon black pepper

1 teaspoon paprika

1/2 tablespoon cooking oil, if using soy chorizo

5 ounces Mexican chorizo, beef, pork, or soy

4 eggs

1/2 cup spicy roasted salsa [see page 18]

Sliced avocado for serving

Sliced jalapeño chile for serving

Chopped fresh cilantro for serving

1. Preheat oven to 350°F.

2. Spray a 5x9 casserole dish with cooking spray. Set aside.

3. Combine shredded potatoes, onion strips, olive oil, salt, pepper, and paprika in a large bowl. Toss with a fork to mix well.

4. Transfer mixture to prepared casserole dish and spread into an even layer.

5. Bake for 25 minutes.

6. While potato mixture bakes, heat a large skillet over medium heat. If you are using soy chorizo, add 1/2 tablespoon cooking oil to warm skillet. Add chorizo and stir, breaking up into crumbs until fully cooked, about 10 minutes. Remove from heat, set aside, and keep warm.

7. Remove casserole from oven. Using a spoon, make four indentations the size of a yolk in baked shredded potatoes. Crack an egg into each indentation.

8. Spoon spicy roasted salsa around each yolk.

9. Return to oven and bake for 25 minutes or until eggs are cooked to your preference.

10. Remove from oven and top with cooked chorizo, avocado, jalapeño, and cilantro. Serve.

MOLLETES

Open-Faced Breakfast Sandwich

Serves 2
Preparation time: 10 minutes
Cooking time: 10 minutes

Molletes *can be enjoyed anytime of the day, but a breakfast* **mollete** *is something to behold. A crispy bolillo vessel loaded with the delicious flavors of Mexican breakfast all in one bite! The basic* **mollete** *of a toasted bolillo smeared with beans and topped with Oaxaca cheese is the base/canvas—how you build upon it is up to you! This is a blueprint of how to make a* **mollete***, but feel free to add your favorite toppings. —Nicole*

2 bolillos

4 teaspoons butter, divided

1/2 cup árbol chile refried pinto beans [see page 164], divided

1 cup shredded Oaxaca cheese, divided

4 eggs, cooked sunny-side up or scrambled, divided

1/2 cup chorizo with potatoes [see page 167], divided

4 teaspoons pico de gallo, divided

Thinly sliced avocado for serving

Hot sauce or salsa for serving

1/8 teaspoon salt

1/8 teaspoon pepper

1. Preheat oven to 450°F.

2. Line a small baking tray with aluminum foil or parchment paper. Set aside.

3. Slice bolillos in half lengthwise.

4. Remove a little bit of bread from the middle of each half to allow for more filling in the middle.

5. Place bolillo slices on baking tray and place in oven for 2 to 3 minutes to allow to toast and brown slightly.

6. Remove from oven and top each half with 1 teaspoon butter, 2 tablespoons refried beans, and 1/4 cup Oaxaca cheese.

7. Place bread back into the oven and bake until cheese melts, about 5 minutes.

8. Remove from oven and top each half with an egg, 2 tablespoons chorizo with potatoes, 1 teaspoon pico de gallo, avocado slices, and hot sauce or salsa.

9. Season with salt and pepper.

10. Two halves per person. Serve hot.

PICADITAS
Breakfast Picaditas

Makes 10
Preparation time: 20 minutes
Cooking time: 25 minutes

I like to think of picaditas as bite-size masa *breakfast cakes that can be eaten quickly and yet carry so much flavor. These simple picaditas are served at breakfast with a smear of salsa (red, green, árbol, or mole), queso fresco, a drizzle of crema, and some onion. —Nicole*

PICADITAS

2 1/4 cups masa harina, divided

1/2 teaspoon salt

1 1/2 cups warm water, divided

TOPPINGS

1 cup vegetable oil

Green salsa [see page 14]

Spicy roasted salsa [see page 18]

1 1/2 cups crumbled queso fresco

1 small white onion, sliced

Crema con sal for serving

1. Mix 2 cups masa harina, salt, and 1 1/3 cups warm water together with your hands until it forms into *masa* (dough). The *masa* should not be crumbly, nor should it stick to your hands. If the *masa* is too wet, add 1 teaspoon at a time of masa harina until it no longer sticks. If the *masa* is crumbly, add 1 teaspoon of warm water at a time until you find a nice medium.

2. On a clean surface, divide the dough into ten equal parts.

3. Hand roll each part into a round ball and place back into the bowl. Cover the bowl with a towel to keep the *masa* from drying out.

4. Preheat a *comal* or griddle over medium-high heat.

5. Line a tortilla press with a plastic sheet on each side. I usually use a clean plastic zip bag (cut to make one long sheet that can line both sides of the tortilla press).

6. Press one *masa* ball in the tortilla press to 1/4-inch thick.

7. Remove the *masa* disk and place it on the heated *comal*. Let the *masa* cook on each side 45 to 50 seconds. The *masa* will begin to inflate.

8. Remove from *comal* and place on a clean work surface. While the *masa* is still warm, grab a napkin or dish rag and use it as a buffer between your fingers and the warm *masa* disk. Start to pinch the edge of the *masa* disk all the way around to create a little rim on your picadita.

9. Place picadita on a plate covered with a towel while you continue pressing and cooking the remaining *masa*.

10. Once all the picaditas are formed, heat vegetable oil in a frying pan over medium heat.

11. Fry each picadita for 2 minutes or until just crisp.

12. Remove from oil and place on a paper towel–lined plate to remove any excess oil.

13. Spread a teaspoon of salsa on the inside belly of the picadita, then add 2 tablespoons queso fresco, a few slices of onion, and a drizzle of crema con sal.

BURRITO DE HUEVO CON NOPALITOS

Cactus and Egg Burrito

Makes 2
Preparation time: 10 minutes
Cooking time: 15 minutes

Adding cactus to your breakfast regularly is a great way to include fiber in your meals. Not only is it healthy, but it's also delicious. Wrap it up in a flour tortilla with chunky pico de gallo and scrambled eggs and you have yourself one of the best Mexican breakfasts around! —Ericka

2 tablespoons cooking oil

1/4 cup white onion, sliced

1 Roma tomato, chopped

1 cup cooked cactus, chopped

1 large jalapeño chile, stem and seeds removed, chopped

1/2 teaspoon salt

4 large eggs, beaten

2 tablespoons fresh cilantro, chopped

1/4 teaspoon black pepper

2 large flour tortillas

Spicy roasted salsa [see page 18] for serving

1. Heat oil in a large skillet over medium heat. Add onion and cook for 3 minutes or until onion begins to soften.

2. Add tomato, cactus, and jalapeño. Season with salt and stir until tomato begins to fall apart, about 7 minutes.

3. Pour in eggs and fold ingredients together until eggs begin to set.

4. Stir in cilantro and pepper. When eggs have set, remove from heat.

5. Warm tortillas over a large skillet or *comal*. When tortillas are soft enough to roll, remove from skillet.

6. Add egg mixture on the center of each tortilla, tuck in the sides, and roll.

7. Return to hot skillet, seam side down, until golden-brown spots appear.

8. Serve with spicy roasted salsa.

TORTITAS DE NOPALES CON QUESO EN CHILE COLORADO

Cactus Patties with Cheese on Chile Colorado

Makes 26
Preparation time: 35 minutes
Cooking time: 25 minutes

For all the cactus lovers out there, this recipe of cactus tortitas *will enchant you at any time of the day. Made with fluffy whisked egg and bits of queso fresco, they sit on a bed of chile colorado. I like to wrap them up in a corn tortilla or enjoy them with a side of rice. Delicious!* —Ericka

CHILE COLORADO

4 cups water

10 dried puya chiles, seeds and veins removed

1 dried pasilla chile, seeds and veins removed

5 dried guajillo chiles, seeds and veins removed

1/3 cup white onion, roughly chopped

2 cloves of garlic

1 teaspoon salt

CACTUS PATTIES

6 eggs, yolks and whites separated

2 cups queso fresco, cubed, plus more crumbled for garnish

2 cups cooked cactus, diced

1/2 teaspoon salt

1/2 teaspoon black pepper

1 cup vegetable oil

Rice for serving

Chile Colorado

1. Bring 4 cups water to a boil over medium heat. Add dried chile skins, boil for 1 minute, turn heat off, and soak for 30 minutes.

2. Transfer 3 cups of chile-boiled water and chiles to blender; add onion, garlic, and salt. Blend until smooth.

3. Run through a fine sieve into a serving bowl. Keep warm.

Cactus Patties

1. In a large bowl, use a hand mixer to beat egg whites to soft peaks.

2. Add yolks, one at a time, until mixed well.

3. Gently fold in cheese, cactus, salt, and pepper.

4. Heat oil in a large skillet over medium heat. Reduce heat to medium-low.

5. Spoon 1/4 cup egg mixture on hot oil, working in batches of 2 or 3 with approximately 1 inch of space between patties. Fry for 1 minute on each side or until golden. Transfer to a paper towel–lined plate. Repeat until all mixture has been used.

6. Pour 1/4 cup chile colorado sauce in a shallow dish, arrange 3 to 4 tortitas over the sauce, and top with crumbled queso fresco.

7. Serve with rice.

QUESO EN SALSA VERDE

Cheese in Green Salsa

Serves 8
Preparation time: 15 minutes
Cooking time: 1 hour 10 minutes

When I make queso en salsa verde, *I like to roast the poblano chiles ahead of time. It saves me so much time in the morning, and this spicy dish comes together quite quickly when prepped in advance. Serve it with fried eggs, beans, tortillas, or tostadas for the full Mexican breakfast experience.* —Ericka

3 large poblano chiles

2 tablespoons cooking oil, divided

3 serrano chiles, stems removed

2 jalapeño chiles, stems removed

2 pounds tomatillos, husks removed

1/2 cup white onion, chopped

2 cloves of garlic

1/2 cup fresh cilantro

1/2 teaspoon salt

2 cups water, divided

1 pound panela cheese, sliced in 1 1/2–inch squares 1/2-inch thick

Cooked pinto beans for serving

Corn tortillas for serving

1. Roast poblanos over an open flame until char spots evenly form on all sides. [See detailed instructions on page 5.] Transfer to a clean plastic zip bag, seal, and let steam for 10 minutes.

2. Carefully remove poblanos from bag. Scrape charred skin off with a spoon or the back of a knife. Remove and dispose of seeds and stem. Set aside poblanos. Heat a *comal* or large skillet over medium-high heat. Place serrano chiles, jalapeños, and tomatillos on *comal*, turning frequently with tongs until char spots appear, about 15 minutes.

3. Transfer to a blender. Add onion, garlic, cilantro, salt, and 3/4 cup water. Blend on medium speed for 10 seconds.

4. Heat 1 teaspoon oil in a separate skillet over medium-high heat. Roast a single layer of cheese slices at a time in the skillet, turning frequently or until golden and charred spots appear, then transfer to a plate.

5. Repeat until all the cheese slices are roasted. Set aside.

6. Heat remaining oil over medium heat in a large sauté pan. Add blended sauce and poblano strips. Add water 1/4 cup at a time if sauce is too thick. Cover and simmer for 10 minutes.

7. Remove from heat, add cheese slices, cover, and let rest for 10 minutes or until cheese slices are heated through.

8. Serve with pinto beans and corn tortillas.

ENMOLADAS DE POLLO
Chicken Mole Folds

Serves 4
Preparation time: 10 minutes
Cooking time: 45 minutes

Enmoladas *are the cousin to enchiladas except with a mole sauce to replace the chile sauce found in enchiladas. This version of mole-coated tortillas is stuffed with shredded chicken for a flavorful break-fast that can be made with leftover mole. Garnish with crema and queso fresco to elevate this meal even further. —Nicole*

1 tablespoon olive oil

1 bay leaf

2 cloves of garlic, slightly crushed

2 tablespoons salt

3 boneless chicken breasts

1/4 cup vegetable oil

8 corn tortillas

2 cups yellow mole [see page 179]

Crema mexicana for serving

Crumbled queso fresco for serving

Eggs for serving

Avocado for serving

1. Fill a medium pot with water and place over high heat. Add olive oil, bay leaf, garlic, and salt. Bring to a boil.

2. Add chicken to boiling water and boil for 20 minutes or until cooked all the way through.

3. Remove chicken from water and place in a bowl. Shred chicken using two forks. This should make 3 cups of chicken. Season to taste.

4. Add 1 tablespoon of cooking water to chicken to keep it moist.

5. In a small frying pan, heat vegetable oil over medium-low heat. Once oil is warmed, fry tortillas one at a time for 45 seconds on each side. Set aside.

6. Add yellow mole to a medium pan over low heat. Once warmed, dip each tortilla in the mole to coat.

7. Fill each tortilla with a heaping 1/3 cup of shredded chicken and fold in half.

8. Repeat until all tortillas are used.

9. Place two chicken-filled tortillas on a plate and pour an additional 1/4 cup yellow mole over the top of the tortillas.

10. Drizzle with crema and queso fresco.

11. Serve with a side of eggs and avocado.

TORTA DE CHILAQUILES
Chilaquiles Sandwich

Makes 4
Preparation time: 10 minutes
Cooking time: 45 minutes

Torta de chilaquiles *is breakfast to many people on the go. This Mexico City classic street-food breakfast can be piled high with a variety of toppings, but the star here is the true standard* chilaquiles rojos *and lots of cotija and crema.*
—Nicole

4 bolillos

8 tablespoons crema mexicana, divided

Red chile chilaquiles [see page 128], divided

1/2 cup crumbled cotija cheese, divided

1/2 cup sliced red onion, divided

1 avocado, sliced thin, divided

1. Slice bolillos lengthwise without cutting all the way through.

2. Smear 2 tablespoons of crema mexicana on the inside of each bolillo, top and bottom.

3. Add one quarter of red chile chilaquiles and sprinkle with 2 tablespoons of cotija cheese.

4. Top with 2 tablespoons of red onion and one quarter of avocado slices.

5. Repeat with remaining ingredients.

TOSTADAS DE HUEVOS REVUELTOS CON RAJAS Y ELOTE

Chile Strips and Corn Scramble on Tostadas

Serves 4–6
Preparation time: 15 minutes
Cooking time: 25 minutes

If you love the flavors of roasted poblano and corn, this is the breakfast for you! With the addition of onion, jalapeño, tomatillo, and queso fresco, this scramble is so delicious, it can be enjoyed on a tostada, in a taco, or in a burrito. —Ericka

2 poblano chiles

1 tablespoon butter

1 tablespoon cooking oil

1/2 cup white onion, finely chopped

1 clove of garlic, finely chopped

1 cup fresh or canned corn

1 large jalapeño chile, stem, seeds, and veins removed

2 large tomatillos, chopped

1/2 teaspoon salt

4 eggs, beaten

2 tablespoons fresh cilantro, finely chopped

1/3 cup queso fresco, cubed

Tostadas or tortillas for serving

1. Roast poblano chiles over an open flame. [See detailed instructions on page 5.] Using tongs, turn to char evenly on all sides.

2. Transfer to a clean plastic zip bag, seal, and steam for 10 minutes.

3. Using the edge of a spoon or the back of a knife, scrape charred skin off.

4. Slice open; remove stems, veins, and seeds; and slice in strips. Set aside.

5. Heat butter and oil in a large skillet over medium heat. When butter melts, add onion and garlic and cook for 1 minute.

6. Slice jalapeño.

7. Add corn and jalapeño strips to the skillet. Cook stirring frequently for 8 minutes or until jalapeño strips soften.

8. Add poblano strips and tomatillos; season with salt. Decrease heat to medium-low and continue cooking for 5 minutes.

9. Add eggs and cilantro. Fold all ingredients and cook until eggs are set.

10. Turn heat off. Fold in queso fresco. Cover and let cheese soften for 5 minutes.

11. Serve on tostadas or wrapped in a tortilla as a taco or burrito.

PAN FRANCÉS DE QUESO COTIJA

Cotija French Toast

Serves 4
Preparation time: 10 minutes
Cooking time: 20 minutes

French toast is usually sweet, drizzled in maple syrup, and decorated with seasonal berries and a dollop of sweet cream. The first time I made this savory cotija French toast, my family lost its mind! It's a buttery treat with crispy, cheesy edges no one can resist. Plus, it's so quick to prep and perfect for those busy mornings. I like to finish it off with a simple side salad to give it a hint of freshness. —Ericka

4 eggs

1/2 cup crumbled cotija cheese, plus more for sprinkling

1/3 cup milk

1/2 teaspoon ground black pepper

1/2 cup butter, divided

8 slices challah bread

Side salad for serving

Crema mexicana or sour cream for serving

1. Whisk together eggs, 1/2 cup cotija cheese, milk, and pepper.

2. Pour mixture into a shallow bowl large enough to fit a slice of challah bread. Set aside.

3. Melt 2 tablespoons butter in a large pan over medium heat.

4. Dip each side of a slice of bread in egg mixture for approximately 30 seconds.

5. Transfer to pan with butter and fry for 2 minutes on each side or until golden brown and edges are crispy.

6. Remove from heat and set aside.

7. Repeat with remaining slices.

8. Serve with a side salad, a sprinkle of crumbled cotija, and crema mexicana or sour cream.

HUEVOS DIVORCIADOS
Divorced Eggs

Serves 2
Preparation time: 5 minutes
Cooking time: 20 minutes

If you can't decide between green or red sauce, then these huevos divorciados, *divorced eggs, are just for you. Roasted and spicy on one side, tangy and zesty on the other. No need to choose because you get both. Serve them with creamy refried beans and enjoy!* —Ericka

1/4 cup cooking oil

4 corn tortillas

4 large eggs

Árbol chile refried pinto beans [see page 164], warmed

Crumbled cotija cheese for serving

2/3 cup green salsa [see page 14], warmed, divided

2/3 cup spicy roasted salsa [see page 18], warmed, divided

Sliced red onion for serving

Chopped fresh cilantro for serving

1. Heat oil in a large skillet over medium heat. Lightly fry tortillas about 1 minute on each side. Transfer to a paper towel–lined plate to absorb excess oil.

2. Crack 1 or 2 eggs at a time into oil and fry, scooping hot oil over yolk.

3. Place two tortillas on a serving plate and top with a fried egg on each.

4. Spoon árbol chile refried pinto beans down the middle between the two yolks and sprinkle with cotija cheese.

5. Repeat with remaining eggs and tortillas.

6. Spoon 1/3 cup green salsa around yolk of one fried egg and 1/3 cup spicy roasted salsa around the other yolk on each plate.

7. Top with red onion slices and cilantro. Serve.

NOPALES RELLENOS DE HUEVO CON CHORIZO

Egg-and-Chorizo-Stuffed Cactus Pads

Serves 4
Preparation time: 15 minutes
Cooking time: 35 minutes

Cactus is so versatile and so good for you! Besides chopping it up in strips and cooking it, I like to save time and cook it stuffed with eggs and chorizo. This breakfast is so festive and hearty. I guarantee your guests will be impressed once they see this delicious spread. Bonus: these can be cooked on the grill too!
—Ericka

1 tube (9 ounces) Mexican chorizo	8 slices Manchego cheese, divided
2/3 cup white onion, chopped, divided	Rice for serving
2 large Roma tomatoes, chopped, divided	Beans for serving
4 eggs	Pico de gallo for serving
8 cactus pads, thorns removed	

1. Heat large skillet over medium heat. Add chorizo and stir, breaking it up with a wooden spoon, for about 2 minutes.

2. Add 1/3 cup onion and half of the chopped tomato. Cook until chorizo is cooked through and onion is tender, about 8 minutes.

3. Add eggs, stirring to mix well; cook until eggs are firm, about 4 minutes. Set aside.

4. On a working surface, place a 12-inch piece of foil. Place one cactus pad on foil; top with 3/4 cup egg and chorizo mixture and two slices of cheese.

5. Cover with another cactus pad.

6. Wrap stuffed cactus pads with foil, overlapping the ends to avoid oil seeping out.

7. Repeat with remaining cactus pads and filling.

8. Heat *comal* or skillet over medium heat. Place cactus foil packets on *comal* and heat for 10 minutes on each side. Use tongs to turn packets.

9. Carefully unwrap packets and place on a serving plate.

10. Serve with rice, beans, and pico de gallo.

TORTA DE HUEVO Y SALCHICHA
Egg and Frankfurter Sandwich

Makes 4
Preparation time: 10 minutes
Cooking time: 15 minutes

This is a great breakfast sandwich to take on an early morning road trip. A comforting meal that can hold you over until lunchtime and can double down as a nice addition to the brunch table. The salchicha *and egg mixture can also be added to a flour tortilla for a delicious burrito!* —Nicole

4 small fresh bolillos

1 teaspoon vegetable oil

4 wieners, beef or plant-based, sliced lengthwise

2 tablespoons butter

6 eggs

8 teaspoons crema mexicana

8 thinly sliced pieces of queso fresco

Pickled jalapeño chile slices (optional)

1. Slice bolillos lengthwise. Set aside.

2. Place pan over medium-high heat; add vegetable oil to coat. Cook frankfurters for 5 minutes on each side. If using plant-based, cook on each side for 2 minutes.

3. While frankfurters are cooking, whisk eggs in a mixing bowl until combined.

4. Remove frankfurters from pan and set aside.

5. In the same pan, melt the butter and then pour in whisked eggs.

6. Cook mixing constantly for 5 minutes or until eggs come together in a scramble. Remove from heat.

7. Smear 2 teaspoons crema mexicana on the inside of each bolillo slice.

8. Divide the scrambled eggs equally among four bolillo slices.

9. Add two pieces of cooked frankfurters to each bolillo slice.

10. Top with two slices of queso fresco, pickled jalapeño slices for a spicy bite, and another bolillo slice.

11. Serve warm.

    Tip: If you only have day-old bolillos, slice them lengthwise and place on a *comal* or hot pan to toast slightly for 2 minutes on each side. This will soften the inside and give your exterior a crunch.

    Note: Some people prefer to slice the frankfurters into 1/2-inch rounds and fry them slightly before adding the whisked eggs and cooking them together. That method works too!

TORTILLA CON HUEVO
Egg with Tortilla

Serves 2–3
Preparation time: 5 minutes
Cooking time: 20 minutes

Tortilla con huevo *seems to have many names attached to its deliciousness. You may know it as* migas, tortillitas, *or* viejas con huevos. *This simple dish is a beloved breakfast for many Mexican families and will keep you coming back for more.* —Nicole

6 corn tortillas

1/4 cup vegetable oil

1/8 teaspoon salt

1/4 cup tomato, chopped

1/4 cup onion, chopped

4 eggs

2 tablespoons crumbled cotija cheese or queso fresco

1 stalk green onion, chopped

1. Cut corn tortillas into small 1/4-inch squares.
2. Add vegetable oil to a large frying pan over medium heat; allow to get hot.
3. Fry the corn tortillas, flipping them often, making them into crisp chips.
4. Remove chips from oil and drain on a paper towel–lined plate. Sprinkle with salt.
5. Drain excess oil from the pan, then place pan back over the heat.
6. Sauté tomato and onion for 3 minutes to soften.
7. Add corn chips and mix completely.
8. In a bowl, whisk eggs and then pour them over the onion/tomato/corn chip mixture.
9. Mix to combine, stirring until eggs are completely cooked.
10. Sprinkle cheese over the top.
11. Serve hot and garnished with green onions.

MACHACA CON HUEVOS
Eggs and Shredded Dried Beef

Serves 4
Preparation time: 5 minutes
Cooking time: 20 minutes

Machaca con huevos *is made of shredded dried beef* (carne seca)*, diced onion, tomato, and jalapeño that is rehydrated in a sauté, then egg is added to the top to make a mouthwatering scramble. This is one of the most popular breakfast dishes in both Mexico and amongst Mexican-Americans living in the United States.* —Nicole

1/4 cup vegetable oil

1/3 cup onion, chopped

1 jalapeño chile, minced

1 Roma tomato, diced

3 1/2 ounces dried machaca meat

8 eggs

Beans for serving

Tortillas for serving

1. Heat oil in a large frying pan over medium heat.

2. Sauté onion and jalapeño for 3 minutes in warm oil.

3. Add chopped tomato and sauté for an additional 5 minutes or until tomatoes soften.

4. Add dried machaca meat and stir to combine with onion mixture. Cook for 5 minutes or until machaca meat is fully hydrated again.

5. In a separate bowl, whisk eggs and then pour them over the machaca mixture. Cook for 5 minutes, mixing together until eggs are set.

6. Serve with beans and warm corn tortillas.

TAMALES FRITOS CON HUEVOS

Fried Tamales with Eggs

Serves 2
Preparation time: 5 minutes
Cooking time: 20 minutes

During Christmastime and at the beginning of the new year, tamales are plentiful. For this breakfast treat, you will need cold tamales that are already steamed. The regular tamal *is then transformed into a crispy* masa *meal topped with an over-easy egg. You may never enjoy a* tamal *any other way. Tip: Any savory* tamal *works with this recipe.*
—Nicole

1 1/2 tablespoons vegetable oil, divided

2 cold tamales, husks removed

2 eggs

Crema con sal for serving

Salsa for serving

1. Heat 1 tablespoon vegetable oil in a non-stick pan over medium-high heat.

2. Add tamales and fry on each side for 5 to 7 minutes or until perfectly crisp and browned.

3. Place on a paper towel–lined plate to remove any excess oil.

4. In the same pan, add 1/2 tablespoon vegetable oil and fry eggs until whites set, about 3 to 5 minutes. You will want to leave the yolk a little runny for this recipe.

5. Transfer tamales to a serving plate, then remove eggs from pan and place an egg over each *tamal*.

6. Serve with crema con sal and salsa for a truly wonderful breakfast!

HOMEMADE TAMALES

Makes 12
Preparation time: 1 hour 30 minutes
Cooking time: 2 hours
Cooling time: 15 minutes

1 package (8 ounces) dried corn husks

10 ounces Oaxaca cheese

MASA

1 cup solid vegetable shortening or lard

1 tablespoon kosher salt

2 teaspoons baking powder

3 1/2 cups masa harina

2 tablespoons dried Mexican oregano

3 cups warm water

RAJAS

3 tablespoons olive oil

4 pasilla chiles

1. Place corn husks in a large tub of hot water. Soak overnight or for a minimum of 4 hours to soften.

2. Cut the cheese into 1/2-inch strips and set aside until ready to use.

Make the *masa*.

1. Place vegetable shortening or lard, salt, and baking powder in a stand mixer and beat until fluffy, about 4 minutes.

2. Scrape mixture down with a rubber spatula. With mixer on low, slowly add masa harina and oregano until fully combined.

3. Turn the speed up on the mixer to high and beat for an additional 2 minutes.

4. Turn mixer speed back to low and pour water into mixture. Continue mixing until combined.

5. Bring the mixer speed back up to high and beat for 5 minutes.

Make the rajas.

1. Pour oil into a small dish. With a pastry brush, generously coat pasilla chiles with olive oil.

2. Place oil-coated pasilla chiles on an open medium-high flame. Burn the skin of the entire chile; it will take about 5 to 7 minutes.

3. Place charred chiles in a plastic zip bag for 20 minutes. This step will allow chiles to steam in their own heat.

4. Remove from zip bag and scrape with a butter knife to remove all charred skin.

5. Remove stems and deseed skinned pasilla chiles.

6. Slice into long strips that are 1/4-inch thick.

7. Remove corn husks from soaking water and shake off/drain. Set aside for assembling.

Assemble the tamales.

1. Place one corn husk on work surface. Take about 1/4 cup of *masa* and spread on the center of a corn husk. Leave a 2-inch frame on the bottom of husk.

2. Place a strip of Oaxaca cheese in the center of *masa*, then top with a few strips of rajas.

3. Fold one long side of husk over the center, then roll to enclose all the *masa*. Fold the bottom end up.

4. Place tamale in a bowl while you prepare the remaining tamales. Keep the open end up so none of the ingredients fall out.

5. Repeat until all tamales are made.

Steam the tamales.

1. Place a rack at the bottom of the steamer pot; pour in water until it is just underneath the rack/grate.

2. Stand the tamales (open end up, folded bottom down) in steamer. Secure empty spaces with wadded husks to prevent tamales from falling over or burning on the pot.

3. Cover the top with remaining corn husks, creating a little insulation over the tamales. Place a few wet kitchen towels over the husks to really lock in the moisture.

4. Place a lid tightly on the steamer and bring the water to a boil over high heat. Steam for 2 hours.

5. Carefully remove a single *tamal* to check if fully cooked. Allow *tamal* to cool for 15 minutes before pulling husk off. If fully cooked, *masa* will pull away from husk easily. If not, cook for an additional 15 minutes or until fully cooked.

CHILAQUILES VERDES CON CHICHARRÓN

Green Chilaquiles with Pork Cracklings

Serves 6–8
Preparation time: 15 minutes
Cooking time: 5 minutes

The best of both worlds: chicharrón en salsa verde *and* chilaquiles. *You get the crunch and the flavor of these two favorites. Top it all with a fried egg and you have yourself a hearty breakfast you are going to love.* —Ericka

3 1/2 cups green salsa [see page 14]

3 cups pork cracklings

1/4 teaspoon salt, or to taste

4 cups tortilla chips

TOPPINGS

Sliced red onion

Sliced jalapeño chile

Crumbled cotija cheese

Chopped fresh cilantro

Crushed dry pork cracklings

6–8 fried eggs, divided

1. Heat green salsa in a large skillet over medium-low heat. Add pork cracklings and salt; simmer for 5 minutes.

2. Fold in tortilla chips.

3. Serve with red onion, jalapeño slices, cotija, cilantro, dry pork cracklings, and a fried egg.

HUEVOS AL COMAL EN HIERBA SANTA

Griddle Eggs on Mexican Pepperleaf

Serves 2
Preparation time: 5 minutes
Cooking time: 5 minutes

This Oaxacan breakfast favorite can be made in minutes. Hierba santa *takes center stage in this recipe with its large leaves serving as the base flavoring to the eggs.* Peppery mint-tasting hierba santa *is grown in Oaxaca, California, and Oregon. It can be found in most Mexican markets or online.* —Nicole

4 leaves Mexican pepperleaf

4 eggs

1/2 teaspoon salt, divided

Refried black beans [see page 176] for serving

Corn tortillas for serving

Queso fresco for serving

Yellow mole [see page 179] for serving

1. Rinse Mexican pepperleaf clean and pat dry.

2. On a hot *comal* or non-stick pan over medium heat, arrange two leaves of Mexican pepperleaf.

3. Crack two eggs directly on top of leaves. Sprinkle 1/8 teaspoon salt on each egg.

4. Allow to cook through until egg whites set, about 5 to 7 minutes. Leaves will wilt slightly.

5. Remove from *comal*.

6. Repeat with remaining Mexican pepperleaf and eggs.

7. Serve with refried black beans, corn tortillas topped with queso fresco, and yellow mole.

HUEVOS CON JAMÓN
Ham and Eggs

Serves 3
Preparation time: 5 minutes
Cooking time: 10 minutes

This simple breakfast is easy to prepare when you only have a few minutes to dedicate to the morning meal. The ham-and-egg combo is delicious on its own, but it is equally as wonderful as a filling for burritos and breakfast tacos or served with pan tostado *(toast).* —Nicole

5 eggs

2 tablespoons vegetable oil

4 slices of ham, cut into 1-inch squares

1 serrano chile, minced

1/3 cup onion, diced

1/8 teaspoon salt

1/8 teaspoon pepper

Refried black beans [see page 176] for serving

Garden salsa [see page 13] for serving

1. Crack eggs into a medium bowl. Whisk eggs until completely scrambled and set aside.

2. Heat oil in a large frying pan over medium heat. Add ham pieces and fry on each side for 2 minutes just to brown.

3. Add serrano chile and onion and sauté for an additional 2 minutes.

4. Pour eggs into the frying pan and mix until eggs are completely cooked through. Season with salt and pepper.

5. Serve with refried black beans and garden salsa.

CHILAQUILES SIN CHILE
No-Chile Chilaquiles

Serves 4–6
Preparation time: 10 minutes
Cooking time: 35 minutes

Chilaquiles don't always have to be spicy. Here's a tamed-down version made with a savory tomato broth that can be enjoyed by the entire family. Kid-friendly and delicious, adults will love it too! —Ericka

5 Roma tomatoes

2 cloves of garlic, unpeeled

1/4 teaspoon dried Mexican oregano

1/4 teaspoon dried basil

1/4 teaspoon ground cumin

1/4 teaspoon dried thyme

1 1/2 teaspoons sea salt

3 cups water, divided

1 1/2 tablespoons + 3/4 cup vegetable oil, divided

2 tablespoons tomato paste

3 cups sliced corn tortillas

Queso fresco for serving

Chopped onions for serving

Crema mexicana or sour cream for serving

Sliced avocado for serving

Chopped cilantro for serving

Black beans for serving

1. Heat *comal* or skillet over medium-high heat. Place tomatoes and garlic on hot skillet and roast, turning frequently with tongs, until char spots form and skins on tomatoes begin to peel. Remove from heat.

2. Let garlic cloves cool to the touch and peel.

3. Place roasted tomatoes, roasted garlic cloves, oregano, basil, cumin, thyme, salt, and 1 cup water in blender. Blend until smooth, approximately 1 minute.

4. Heat 1 1/2 tablespoons oil in a medium saucepan over medium heat. Add blended tomatoes, 2 cups water, and tomato paste. Simmer for 15 minutes, stirring occasionally.

5. While sauce simmers, heat 3/4 cup vegetable oil in a large frying pan over medium heat. Working in batches, add 1 cup tortilla pieces and fry until golden and crispy. Transfer to a paper towel–lined plate before frying the next batch.

6. To serve, place desired quantity of fried tortilla chips on a shallow serving plate. Top with desired quantity of sauce, queso fresco, onions, crema mexicana, avocado, and cilantro. Serve with a side of black beans.

CARNE DE CERDO CON CHILE COLORADO

Pork Chile Colorado

Serves 4
Preparation time: 15 minutes
Cooking time: 1 hour 10 minutes

If you are looking for a spicy version of chile colorado, then you've come to the right place. With the addition of dried puya chiles, this recipe goes from mild to a delicious kick. Don't like spicy? Replace puya chiles with guajillo. This hearty breakfast is best served with rice and tortillas. —Ericka

10 1/2 cups water, divided

8 dried guajillo chiles, wiped clean

2 dried puya chiles, wiped clean

2 dried pasilla chiles, wiped clean

3 pounds pork shoulder or pork stew meat, chopped into 1-inch pieces

2 teaspoons salt, divided

1/4 teaspoon whole cumin

1 1/2 teaspoons dried oregano

4 cloves of garlic

1/2 tablespoon cooking oil

2 teaspoons all-purpose flour

Rice for serving

Sliced radishes for serving

1. Bring 6 cups water to a boil in a medium saucepan.

2. While the water comes to a boil, remove seeds and stems from guajillo chiles, puya chiles, and pasilla chiles.

3. Add chile skins to boiling water and turn heat off and let chiles soak for 15 minutes.

4. While chile skins hydrate, add pork meat to a large stockpot over low heat, season with 1 teaspoon salt, and add 1/3 cup water; stir and cover. Cook for 20 minutes, stirring regularly to avoid meat sticking to the bottom of the pan.

5. After 20 minutes, uncover and increase temperature to medium and continue cooking for 10 more minutes until most liquid has evaporated. Set aside.

6. In the meantime, add 1 teaspoon salt, cumin, oregano, garlic, and 1/3 cup water to a blender; blend until smooth.

7. Add soaked chile skins and 1 1/2 cups water and blend again until smooth.

8. Strain sauce through a fine mesh into a bowl. Set aside.

9. Add oil to pork. Cook for 5 minutes over medium-high heat, stirring rapidly until edges begin to crisp.

10. Stir in flour until it dissolves.

11. Add sauce and cook for 3 minutes.

12. Add 2 cups water, lower heat to medium-low, stir thoroughly, and cook for 25 more minutes uncovered.

13. Serve with rice and sliced radishes.

CHICHARRÓN EN SALSA VERDE

Pork Cracklings in Green Salsa

Serves 6–8
Preparation time: 15 minutes
Cooking time: 5 minutes

Pork cracklings, or chicharrones, *are usually found in the prepared food section of the Latin grocery store. Depending on your taste, you have the option of using the pork skins or pork skins with meat. Both are tasty and soften perfectly in this tomatillo salsa. Serve* chicharrón en salsa verde *as a side to your breakfast eggs or as the star of the breakfast table.* —Ericka

3 1/2 cups green salsa [see page 14]

3 cups pork cracklings (with or without meat)

1/4 teaspoon salt, or to taste

Cooked rice for serving

Warm corn tortillas for serving

1. Heat green salsa in a large skillet over medium-low heat.

2. Add pork cracklings; simmer for 10 minutes or until pork crackling soften and are heated through. Season with salt.

3. Serve with rice and corn tortillas.

GORDITAS DE PAPA CON CHORIZO

Potato and Chorizo Flour Gorditas

Makes 24–26
Preparation time: 45 minutes
Cooking time: 50 minutes

Gorditas are a symbol of Torreon, Coahuila, where I was born. My favorite are stuffed with potato and chorizo. They are fluffy, spicy, and so delicious! You can also fill them with frijoles negros refritos *or* frijoles pintos refritos con chile de árbol *[see pages 176 and 164, respectively],* chicharrón en salsa verde *[see page 123], or* tortitas de nopales con queso en chile colorado *[see page 87]. —Ericka*

4 cups all-purpose flour	4 cups russet potatoes, peeled
1 teaspoon salt	6 ounces chorizo (beef, pork, or soy)
1 teaspoon baking powder	1 tablespoon cooking oil (if needed)
1/2 cup vegetable shortening or lard	1/3 cup white onion, chopped
1 1/2 cups warm water	Refried beans for serving

1. Whisk together flour, salt, and baking powder in a large bowl.

2. Add vegetable shortening (or lard) and mix with hands until a mixture resembling sand forms.

3. Add warm water, 1/4 cup at a time, mixing with hands between additions until dough is smooth and not sticky. (Depending on the environment, you might not use all the water or you might need a bit more). Cover with a clean kitchen towel and let rest for 30 minutes.

4. While dough rests, place potatoes in a large saucepan over medium heat with enough water to cover. Boil for 15 minutes, drain, and set aside.

5. When slightly cooled, chop into bite-size pieces.

6. If using soy chorizo, place 1 tablespoon cooking oil in a large skillet. If using beef or pork chorizo, no oil is needed. Cook chorizo for 7 to 10 minutes, stirring frequently or until chorizo is cooked through and broken up into crumbles.

7. Add onion and cook for 5 minutes, stirring until onion is tender but not brown.

8. Stir in potatoes, lightly mashing with a wooden spoon or potato masher, season to taste, and mix for 2 minutes. Remove from heat and cover to keep warm.

9. Preheat a *comal* or skillet over medium heat.

10. Knead dough and divide into 24 balls. Keep covered to avoid drying out.

11. Roll out a dough ball into a 3-inch disc, 1/4-inch thick.

12. Gently place on hot *comal* and cook for 45 to 60 seconds on each side or until golden brown spots form.

13. Remove from heat and transfer to a basket or plate covered with a clean kitchen towel to keep warm.

14. Repeat with the rest of the dough.

15. Using a small knife, make a slit along the side and halfway through each gordita.

16. Smear the inside with refried beans and fill with potato mixture. Serve.

HUEVOS RANCHEROS

Rancher's Eggs

Serves 4
Preparation time: 10 minutes
Cooking time: 20 minutes

A plate of huevos rancheros *is always welcome no matter what time of day. Make the spicy roasted salsa and pinto beans ahead of time and this breakfast will come together in a matter of minutes.* —Ericka

2 tablespoons cooking oil

4 corn tortillas

1/2 cup árbol chile refried pinto beans [see page 164], warmed

4 eggs

Spicy roasted salsa [see page 18] for serving

Crumbled queso fresco for serving

Chopped fresh cilantro for serving

Sliced avocado for serving

1. Heat oil in a large non-stick skillet over medium heat. Fry tortillas, one at a time, about 30 seconds on each side. Transfer to a paper towel–lined plate to absorb excess oil.

2. Place each tortilla on a serving plate. Spread 2 tablespoons of refried beans on each tortilla.

3. In the same skillet, fry eggs to your liking.

4. Place an egg on top of bean layer of each tortilla.

5. Top with spicy roasted salsa, a sprinkle of queso fresco, cilantro, and sliced avocado.

CHILAQUILES ROJOS

Red Chile Chilaquiles

Serves 4
Preparation time: 10 minutes
Cooking time: 45 minutes

Chilaquiles rojos *are a combination of crispy tortilla chips, tasty* salsa roja, *and salty cotija cheese. They are best when the crunchy concoction is served with a fried egg on top. They can be enjoyed anytime of the day but are mostly served at breakfast time.* —Nicole

1 white onion, cut in half

2 1/2 ounces New Mexico chile

6 cloves of garlic

2 1/2 ounces California chile

2 pasilla-ancho chiles

1 tablespoon salt

5 cups water

3/4 cup vegetable oil

20 corn tortillas, each cut into eighths

1/2 cup crumbled cotija cheese

1/4 small red onion, sliced

4 fried eggs

1 radish, sliced

4 sprigs cilantro

1. Boil onion, New Mexico chile, garlic, California chile, pasilla-ancho chiles, and salt in water until chiles soften, about 35 minutes.

2. Remove chiles from water and discard stems and seeds.

3. Transfer all chile skins, onion, garlic, and 3 cups of boiled chile water to a blender. Blend until smooth.

4. Pour chile sauce mixture through a sieve and into a bowl. Press chile flesh against sieve with the back of a spoon to squeeze out all the liquid. Discard any seeds and skin collected in sieve. Place this chile rojo sauce to the side until ready to use.

5. Add vegetable oil to a large frying pan over medium heat and allow to get hot.

6. Working in batches, add tortilla triangles to frying pan. Fry on either side until hard, crisp, and golden, about 2 1/2 minutes on each side.

7. Remove from pan and place in a paper towel–lined bowl to drain.

8. Repeat with remaining tortilla triangles until all are fried. Set aside.

9. Discard most of remaining oil from pan, leaving a tablespoon of vegetable oil in pan.

10. Place pan back on medium heat and pour 1 1/2 cups *chile rojo* in pan to heat.

11. Pour tortilla chips over *chile rojo* and then mix to combine. Allow to cook for 3 minutes.

12. Sprinkle the top with cotija cheese and red onion slices.

13. Plate and garnish with a fried egg, radish slices, and cilantro.

HUEVOS REVUELTOS CON NOPALITOS EN CHILE COLORADO

Scrambled Eggs and Cactus in Red Chile Sauce

Serves 6
Preparation time: 20 minutes
Cook time: 15 minutes

Wake up to this family-style dish of scrambled eggs and cactus cooked in a rich red sauce. This three-chile sauce of guajillo, ancho, and árbol chile might sound spicy, but you'll be surprised at how smokey and mild it is. Serve with a side of refried beans, corn, or flour tortillas and a sweet café de olla [see page 43] to start off your day. —Ericka

4 dried guajillo chiles

1 small dried chile ancho

2 dried árbol chiles

2 cloves of garlic

1/2 teaspoon dried oregano

1 teaspoon salt

2 cups water

1 tablespoon cooking oil

3/4 cup white onion, sliced

2 cups chopped cactus, cooked

6 large eggs, beaten

Corn tortillas for serving

1. Clean all dried chiles with a damp paper towel. Using kitchen shears, cut off stems and cut open chiles to remove seeds.

2. Place guajillo chile skins and ancho chile skin in a large bowl. Fill with enough hot water to cover and soak for 15 minutes or until chile skins are soft.

3. Place soaked chile skins, árbol chile skins, garlic, oregano, salt, and 2 cups water in a blender. Blend until smooth.

4. Run sauce through a mesh sieve and set aside.

5. Heat oil in a large pan over medium-low heat. Add onion and cook for 2 minutes.

6. Add cactus and cook for 3 minutes, stirring frequently.

7. Fold in eggs and gently stir to scramble.

8. When eggs have set, add sauce. Stir and cook for 8 to 10 minutes or until eggs have completely cooked through.

9. Serve with warm corn tortillas.

BOLILLOS RELLENOS

Stuffed Bolillos

Makes 6 large or 12 small
Preparation time: 20 minutes
Cooking time: 1 hour 5 minutes

Have extra vegetables in your refrigerator? Make bolillos rellenos. *Perfect for a large crowd, no silverware is needed, and cleanup is a breeze. Add bacon, chorizo, or sausage for a meat lovers' version.*
—*Ericka*

1 tablespoon cooking oil

2 Yukon Gold potatoes, peeled and diced (about 1 1/2 cups)

1/2 cup white onion, finely chopped

2 large jalapeño chiles, finely chopped

1 orange bell pepper, finely chopped

2 cups spinach, chopped

1/2 teaspoon salt

1/4 teaspoon black pepper

1 large Roma tomato, finely chopped

12 small or 6 large bolillos

1/2 cup butter, room temperature, divided

12 eggs (6 if using large bolillos)

3/4 cup shredded Oaxaca cheese

1/2 teaspoon dried crushed oregano

1/4 teaspoon garlic powder

1. Preheat oven to 375°F.

2. Heat oil in a large skillet over medium heat. Add potatoes and stir. Cook for 12 minutes.

3. Add onion, jalapeños, and bell pepper; cook for 5 minutes.

4. Stir in spinach, salt, and pepper. Cook for 15 minutes or until potatoes are soft and cooked through. Remove from heat.

5. Stir in chopped tomato.

6. Make a slice on each bolillo lengthwise, about 3-inches long. Remove the inside crumb as much as possible and brush the inside with butter (optional).

7. Brush the bottom and sides of a large cast-iron skillet (if using small bolillos) or a baking tray (if using large bolillos) with butter.

8. Fill each bolillo halfway with vegetable mixture.

9. Brush the outside of each bolillo with butter and place in the cast-iron pan or baking tray.

10. Repeat with remaining bolillos and vegetable mixture.

11. Beat one egg at a time and pour into each bolillo.

12. Top with cheese.

13. Sprinkle filled bolillos with oregano and garlic powder.

14. Bake for 30 to 35 minutes or until egg is set and cheese has melted. Serve.

TORTA DE TRES HUEVOS
CON CHILE POBLANO Y CHAMPIÑONES
Three-Egg Poblano Mushroom Omelet

Serves 1
Preparation time: 30 minutes
Cook time: 15 minutes

This is a hearty fancy breakfast for one. It's a great way to use up a leftover poblano chile and add a mild spicy flavor to your omelet. It can also be shared among two people with smaller appetites. —Nicole

1 poblano chile

1 tablespoon olive oil

1/4 large onion, sliced thin

6 mushrooms, cut into 1/8-inch slices

1/4 teaspoon salt

1/8 teaspoon pepper

3 eggs

1 tablespoon crema con sal

1 teaspoon butter

Sliced avocado for serving

Sliced queso fresco for serving

1. Roast poblano chile on an open flame until charred completely. [See detailed instructions on page 5.]

2. Place poblano in a plastic zip bag to steam in its own heat for 20 minutes.

3. Remove from bag and peel off charred skin from the chile under a slow stream of water. Discard stem and slice chile into 2-inch long, 1/8-inch thin strips. Set aside.

4. Add oil to a large frying pan over medium-high heat. Add poblano chile strips and sauté for 5 minutes, mixing occasionally.

5. Add onion and mushrooms to poblano chile mixture and cook for 5 more minutes or until onions look limp and mushrooms are seared. Season with salt and pepper. Remove mixture from pan and set aside.

6. Whisk eggs and crema con sal together in a bowl. Make sure to beat until slightly frothy, this will make for a fluffy omelet.

7. Melt butter in a 9-inch frying pan over medium-high heat.

8. Pour egg mixture into melted butter. Swirl pan to ensure egg reaches the entire diameter of pan. Cook for 2 minutes or until egg sets, then flip the egg over and cook for an additional 1 to 2 minutes, depending how you like your egg cooked.

9. Spoon poblano-mushroom mixture over half of the egg, then fold the other half over the mixture to cover/envelop it.

10. Remove from pan and season with salt and pepper.

11. Serve with avocado and queso fresco slices.

CHILAQUILES GÜEROS
Yellow Chile Chilaquiles

Serves 4
Preparation time: 5 minutes
Cooking time: 30 minutes

Chilaquiles güeros *are best when the tortilla is cooked extra crispy. No one likes a soggy chilaquiles and don't let anyone tell you otherwise. The unique* salsa de chile güero *is a thicker sauce that clings to the crispy chips, giving breakfast an alternative from the typical red or green chilaquiles.* —Nicole

3/4 cup vegetable oil

20 corn tortillas, each cut into eighths

2 cups yellow chile salsa, smooth [see page 21]

1/2 cup crumbled cotija cheese

1/3 cup chopped red onion

2 tablespoons chopped cilantro

1/4 cup crema mexicana

4 fried eggs

1. Add vegetable oil to a large frying pan over medium heat and allow to get hot.

2. Working in batches, add tortilla triangles to frying pan. Do not overcrowd the pan. Giving each piece of tortilla space will allow for extra crispy tortilla pieces. Fry on either side until hard, crisp, and golden, about 3 minutes on each side.

3. Remove from pan and place in a paper towel-lined bowl to drain.

4. Repeat with remaining tortilla triangles until all are fried. Set aside.

5. Discard most of remaining oil from pan, leaving a tablespoon of vegetable oil in pan.

6. Place pan back on medium heat and pour yellow chile salsa in pan to heat.

7. Pour tortilla chips over salsa and mix to combine. Cook for 6 minutes.

8. Sprinkle the top with cotija cheese and chopped red onion.

9. Garnish with cilantro and crema mexicana.

10. Serve with fried eggs.

SWEET MAIN

Entradas Dulces

PAN FRANCES DE PLÁTANO AL RON

Banana Rum French Toast

Serves 5
Preparation time: 15 minutes
Cooking time: 35 minutes

This is a decadent breakfast that can be served for a brunch on a special occasion or for a small gathering of family. Made with a banana loaf French toast base—then topped with a medley of caramelized bananas, whipped cream, fresh berries, and a drizzle of honey—this breakfast pairs beautifully with café de olla or café with lots of crema! —Nicole

BANANA RUM FRENCH TOAST

1 banana rum loaf [see page 189]

1 cup milk

2 eggs

1 tablespoon sugar

1/2 teaspoon Mexican vanilla

1/8 teaspoon ground cinnamon

10 teaspoons butter, divided

CARAMELIZED BANANAS

2 bananas, sliced in 1/4-inch rounds

2 tablespoons brown sugar, packed

1/2 tablespoon butter

1 tablespoon rum

WHIPPED CREAM

1/2 cup heavy whipping cream

2 tablespoons sugar

TOPPINGS

Sliced almonds

Fresh strawberries

Fresh blueberries

Honey

1. Cut banana rum loaf into ten 1-inch slices.

2. Whisk milk, eggs, sugar, vanilla, and cinnamon together in a mixing bowl.

3. Warm a non-stick skillet over medium heat.

4. Dip one banana loaf slice quickly in milk/egg mixture. Remove from mixture and allow excess to drip off.

5. Fry each slice of banana loaf in 1 teaspoon of butter for 2 minutes on each side or until golden crisp.

6. Remove from heat and set aside.

7. Repeat until all pieces are fried.

Make the caramelized bananas.

1. Dip each banana slice in sugar to coat.

2. Heat butter in non-stick skillet until completely melted over medium heat.

3. Add banana slices and fry on both sides for 2 minutes or until crisp and golden.

4. Drizzle in rum and cook until it evaporates, about 30 seconds.

Make the whipped cream.

1. Pour whipping cream into a stand mixer with whisk attachment.

2. Whisk on high for **3** minutes or until soft peaks form, then sprinkle in sugar while cream is still whisking. Whisk for an additional minute.

3. Assemble on plates topped with caramelized bananas, whipped cream, sliced almonds, berries, and a drizzle of honey.

CEREAL DE CEREZA CON ALMENDRA Y AMARANTO

Cherry Almond Amaranth Cereal

Serves 2
Preparation time: 5 minutes
Cooking time: 35 minutes

Amaranth is considered a super food for its many health benefits; this warm bowl of cereal is rich in protein, high in fiber, and gluten-free. The cherries and almonds add to the delicious nutty flavor of the amaranth. It's a great way to lower your cholesterol and reduce inflammation. It is considered one of the world's ancient food crops and was heavily enjoyed by the Aztecs and Incas. —Nicole

2 cups water

4 ounces piloncillo

1 teaspoon vanilla

3 cups milk, whole, evaporated, oat, or almond

Pinch of salt

2 cups amaranth

1/2 cup chopped almonds

1/2 cup pitted and halved cherries

1. In a small saucepan over medium-high heat, bring water, piloncillo, and vanilla to a boil. Allow piloncillo to dissolve completely, about 5 minutes.

2. Add milk, salt, and amaranth. Mix to combine.

3. Once mixture starts to boil again, lower heat to low and simmer cereal for 30 minutes or until mixture thickens. Stir occasionally to prevent amaranth from sticking to the bottom of the pan.

4. Mix in almonds and cherries.

5. Serve immediately.

PAN FRANCÉS CON CHURROS

Churro French Toast

Serves 7–8
Preparation time: 25 minutes
Cooking time: 40 minutes

Transform stale bread into a welcomed feast of churro French toast. Crunchy churros top cinnamon-laced French toast and are accompanied by a bevy of berries. Sprinkle with powdered sugar and garnish with flowers to make it extra special. —Nicole

FRENCH TOAST

1 cup half-and-half or whipping cream

2 eggs

2 tablespoons sugar

1 teaspoon Mexican vanilla

1/4 teaspoon ground cinnamon

15 slices stale bread, cut in half diagonally

3 tablespoons butter

CHURROS

1 cup water

2 tablespoons sugar

3 tablespoons salted butter

1 cup + 2 tablespoons flour

1 egg + 1 egg yolk

3/4 cup vegetable oil

1/4 cup sugar

1 teaspoon ground cinnamon

TOPPINGS

Strawberries

Blackberries

Blueberries

Raspberries

Powdered Sugar

Maple Syrup

Make the French toast.

1. Whisk half-and-half, eggs, sugar, vanilla, and cinnamon together in a mixing bowl.

2. Warm a non-stick skillet over medium heat.

3. Quickly dip each triangle of bread in milk/egg mixture, just enough to barely coat it. Allow excess to drip off.

4. Fry each piece of bread in 1 teaspoon of butter for 2 minutes on each side or until golden crisp.

5. Remove from heat and set aside.

6. Repeat until all pieces are fried. Several slices can be fried at once, just make sure to not overcrowd pan.

Make the churros.

1. In a small saucepan, combine water, sugar, and butter over medium heat. Bring mixture to boil then quickly remove from heat.

2. Stir in flour with a rubber spatula until mixture forms a ball.

3. Place mixture in a stand mixer and allow to cool for 10 to 15 minutes.

4. Mix in egg and egg yolk until dough comes together. Set aside.

5. In a saucepan, heat enough oil to fill over 1 1/2 inches deep. Bring the temperature to 375°F using a candy thermometer.

6. Line a plate with a paper towel.

7. Fit a star-shaped tip (size 1M) inside of a pastry bag. Place the dough inside of the bag and squeeze out 3-inch-long strips into the heated oil. Fry until golden, about 3 minutes.

8. Remove from oil using a slotted spoon and drain on prepared paper towel–lined plate for a few minutes.

9. Mix sugar and cinnamon together with a fork in a bowl.

10. Sprinkle warm churros with sugar-cinnamon mixture until completely coated. You can also roll the churros in the mixture.

11. Divide French toast and churros equally among serving plates.

12. Top with berries, a sprinkle of powdered sugar, and a drizzle of syrup.

HOTCAKES DE ELOTE
Corn Pancakes

Makes 8
Preparation time: 10 minutes
Cooking time: 30 minutes

Start off your morning with a delicious stack of pancakes made with corn. They are not only tasty, but they are quick and easy to prepare in the blender. If fresh corn is not available, canned corn works just as well. Top them with sweetened condensed milk and plump raspberries for a tart finish. —Ericka

1 1/2 cups fresh white corn kernels

3/4 cup all-purpose flour, plus more if needed

3/4 cup milk

1 egg

1 tablespoon butter, room temperature

1 teaspoon vanilla extract

1/2 teaspoon baking soda

1 tablespoon baking powder

1/4 teaspoon ground cinnamon

1/8 teaspoon salt

TOPPING

Raspberries

Fresh corn kernels

Sweetened condensed milk

1. Combine all ingredients in a blender. Blend for **45** seconds or until smooth.

2. Set aside for 10 minutes. If mixture is runny, add 1 to 2 tablespoons flour and mix at low speed.

3. Heat non-stick skillet over medium heat. Spray with non-stick cooking spray or coat with butter.

4. Lower heat to medium-low. Spoon 1/3 cup batter onto skillet. Pancake will bubble. When most bubbles have popped, flip pancake to cook other side, about 1 minute on each side or until golden.

5. Transfer to serving plate and repeat with remaining batter.

6. Serve with raspberries, a few corn kernels, and a drizzle of sweetened condensed milk.

CREPAS CON CAJETA Y NUEZ
Crepes with Cajeta and Pecans

Makes 8–10
Preparation time: 10 minutes
Resting time: 35 minutes
Cooking time: 20 minutes

Sweet and savory crepes were regularly served for breakfast in my home growing up. They are made quickly in a blender and call for few and readily available ingredients. The toppings can vary, but our favorites are cajeta, pecans, and a sprinkle of confectioner's sugar. This recipe can be modified into a savory version by omitting sugar and vanilla extract and topping with ingredients such as ham, cheese, and sautéed mushrooms. —Ericka

1 cup all-purpose flour

2 eggs, room temperature

1 cup 2% milk

3 tablespoons butter, melted and cooled to room temperature

1 1/2 tablespoons granulated sugar

1 teaspoon vanilla extract

1/8 teaspoon salt

1/3 cup water

TOPPINGS

Goat milk caramel [see page 190] or *dulce de leche*

Finely chopped pecans

Confectioner's sugar

1. Combine flour, eggs, milk, butter, sugar, vanilla, salt, and water in a blender. Blend until smooth.

2. Refrigerate mixture for 35 minutes.

3. Heat a 10-inch non-stick pan over medium heat. Spray with non-stick cooking spray or grease with butter.

4. Scoop 1/3 cup batter onto pan and swirl, coating the bottom of the pan with an even layer. Cook for 40 to 45 seconds or until golden spots form. Flip the crepe and cook for 20 seconds.

5. Transfer to a large plate and cover with aluminum foil loosely to keep warm.

6. Repeat with remaining batter.

7. To serve, fold each crepe in fourths.

8. Place 2 to 3 crepes on a serving plate. Drizzle with *cajeta*, sprinkle with pecans, and dust with confectioner's sugar.

AVENA MEXICANA
Mexican Oatmeal

Serves 4
Preparation time: 5 minutes
Cooking time: 15 minutes

During my elementary school days on snowy winter mornings in El Paso, Texas, my mother would let me wear my waffle-knit pajama bottoms under my pants to keep warm. The snow in El Paso wasn't white and fluffy. It was wet, slushy, and bone-chilling. The pajamas under my corduroy pants shielded the soggy snow from seeping entirely through my clothes.

To keep me warm inside, my mom made a big steaming bowl of avenita (sweet Mexican oatmeal). She sweetened it with sugar and raisins and kept it creamy and comforting with milk, pecans, pepitas, and a sprinkle of cinnamon. I'm so happy I was able to include it in this book. This is by far one of my most nostalgic breakfasts. —Ericka

2 cups water

1 cinnamon stick

1 orange peel

1 cup old-fashioned rolled oats

1/8 teaspoon salt

2 cups milk

1 tablespoon pure cane sugar, or to taste

Chopped pecans for serving

Raisins for serving

Raw pepitas for serving

Ground cinnamon for serving

1. Combine water, cinnamon stick, and orange peel in a medium saucepan over medium-high heat. Bring to a boil.

2. Stir in oats and salt and decrease heat to medium; simmer for 5 minutes. Add milk and cook for another 5 minutes.

3. Remove from heat and stir in sugar.

4. Remove cinnamon stick and orange peel.

5. Divide between four bowls and garnish with pecans, raisins, pepitas, and a sprinkle of cinnamon.

CABALLEROS POBRES

Poor Gentlemen

Serves 6
Preparation time: 10 minutes
Cooking time: 20 minutes
Baking time: 40 minutes
Cooling time: 5 minutes

This French toast–like dish originated in the Yucatan. I think of it as a cross between French toast and a capirotada (bread pudding). It is enjoyed as a warm breakfast meal topped with fruit. It can also be served room temperature as a dessert with a scoop of ice cream on the side. —Nicole

PILONCILLO SYRUP

1 cup water

8 ounces piloncillo

1 cinnamon stick

1/2 cup chopped almonds

1 clove

CABALLEROS POBRES

1 cup milk

2 tablespoons sugar

1 teaspoon vanilla extract

3–5 stale mini bolillos (2 days old), sliced 2-inches thick

5 eggs, separated

1 cup vegetable oil

TOPPING

Mango

Shredded sweetened coconut

Piloncillo Syrup

1. Add water, piloncillo, cinnamon stick, chopped almonds, and clove to a small saucepan over medium heat. Allow to simmer until all sugar is melted and completely dissolved.

2. Remove cinnamon stick and clove. Set aside.

Caballeros Pobres

1. Whisk milk, sugar, and vanilla to combine.

2. Dip slices of bolillos into milk batter, then place on a rack to drain excess milk.

3. Whisk egg whites on high speed in a stand mixer until soft peaks form. Mix in egg yolks slowly until just combined.

4. Heat vegetable oil in a frying pan over medium-low heat. Dip each bolillo slice in the egg mixture and then cook in pan for 4 minutes on each side or until golden brown.

5. Place on a paper towel–lined plate to drain.

6. Preheat oven to 350°F.

7. Place a single layer of fried bread at the bottom of a baking dish. Then pour half of piloncillo syrup on the layer. Top with another layer of fried bread. Pour remaining piloncillo syrup over the top.

8. Bake for 35 minutes. Allow to cool for 5 minutes.

9. Top with pieces of mango and shredded sweetened coconut and serve.

BUDÍN DE PAN DULCE

Sweet Bread Pudding

Serves 12
Preparation time: 10 minutes
Baking time: 55 minutes

Budín de pan dulce *is a great way to use up stale* pan dulce. *It can be prepped the night before and baked in the morning before serving. This delicious bread pudding is served warm or cold and is a perfect addition to Sunday brunch.* —Nicole

2 tablespoons butter

10 cups *pan dulce* variety (about 6 regular-sized pastries),
  two days old

8 eggs

2 cups milk

1/4 cup brown sugar, packed

1/4 cup sugar

1 tablespoon vanilla

1/8 teaspoon salt

1. Preheat oven to 350°F.

2. Grease a 2.5-quart baking dish with butter and set aside.

3. Cut *pan dulce* into different-sized pieces, some 1-inch cubes and others in strips to fit into the baking dish like a puzzle. Reserve any crumb toppings for later use.

4. Whisk eggs, milk, brown sugar, sugar, vanilla, and salt together in a large mixing bowl.

5. Pour 2 cups of egg mixture into the bottom of prepared baking dish.

6. Spread the *pan dulce* pieces over the egg mixture, layering the larger pieces on top.

7. Carefully pour the remaining egg mixture over the top. Press down on the *pan dulce* to make sure all the pieces are soaking in wet mixture.

8. Loosely cover top of baking dish with aluminum foil and bake for 40 minutes.

9. Remove the aluminum foil and continue baking for an additional 15 minutes.

10. Remove from oven and sprinkle any crumb toppings from *pan dulce* over the top.

WAFLES DE TRES LECHES
Three-Milk Waffles

Makes 6
Preparation time: 15 minutes
Cooking time: 30 minutes

Buenos días *means "good day," and it certainly will be when it starts with a plate of* tres leches *waffles. The crispy waffle soaks up the sweet* tres leches *mixture for the most delicious creamy bite. Dust with ground cinnamon and a little whipped cream and you'll have a slice of happiness on your plate.* —Nicole

3 cups all-purpose flour

2 tablespoons baking powder

1/8 teaspoon salt

2 1/2 cups whole milk

3 eggs

3/4 cup butter, melted

3 tablespoons sugar

1 tablespoon vanilla

1/2 cup sweetened condensed milk

1/2 cup evaporated milk

1/2 cup heavy cream

Fruit for serving

Whipped cream for serving

Ground cinnamon for serving

1. Preheat waffle iron as directed by manufacturer's instructions.

2. In a large mixing bowl, whisk flour, baking powder, and salt together to combine.

3. In a separate bowl, whisk milk, eggs, butter, sugar, and vanilla together until sugar dissolves.

4. Combine dry ingredients with wet ingredients, making sure not to overmix.

5. Spray inside of waffle iron with a non-stick spray, then pour 1/2 cup waffle batter into the center of the waffle iron.

6. Close the lid and cook for 4 to 5 minutes or until perfectly browned.

7. Remove from waffle iron by using a long wooden stick (kabob stick) or plastic tongs.

8. In a separate bowl, whisk sweetened condensed milk, evaporated milk, and heavy cream together; pour over waffles.

9. Serve with fruit, whipped cream, and a dusting of ground cinnamon.

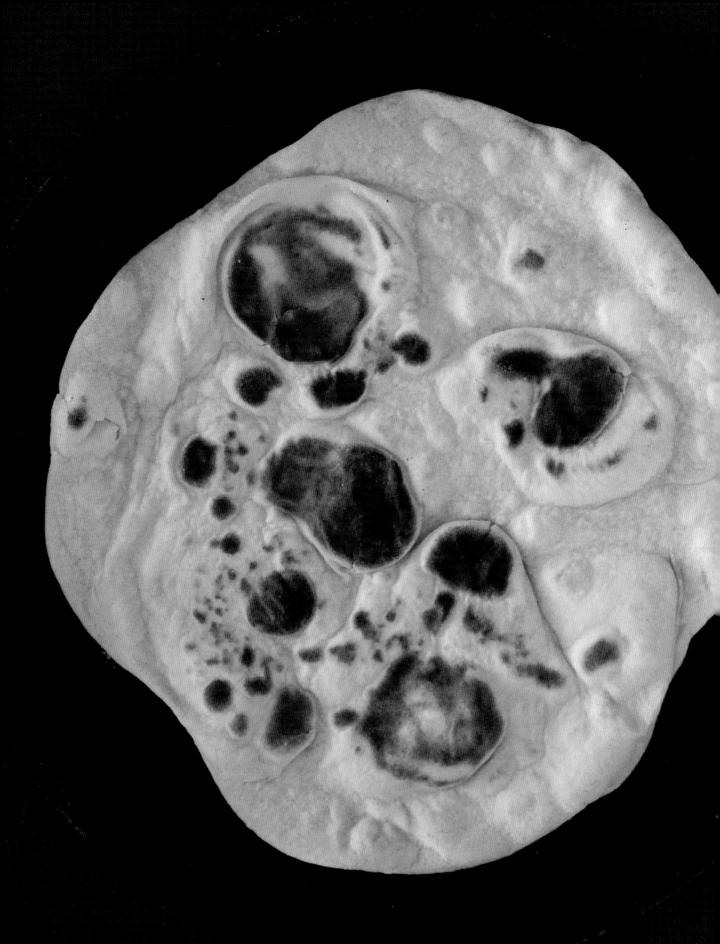

SIDES

Guarniciones

FRIJOLES PINTOS REFRITOS
CON CHILE DE ÁRBOL
Árbol Chile Refried Pinto Beans

Serves 10
Preparation time: 15 minutes
Cooking time: 4 hours 15 minutes

Refried beans are a staple to many dishes. There is a welcome space for beans on the plate any time of the day, and breakfast is no different. What makes these beans so special is in the preparation. Make sure to smash the beans first and then add the liquid. This recipe will produce the creamiest beans!
—Nicole

1 pound dry pinto beans	1 bay leaf
11 1/2 cups water, divided	4 árbol chiles, divided
1/2 medium white onion	6 tablespoons olive oil, divided
8 cloves of garlic, divided	1/2 tablespoon salt

1. Sort through dry beans and remove any little rocks or cracked beans.

2. Place beans in a sieve and rinse thoroughly under warm water, rubbing them between your hands to clean them of any dirt or debris.

3. Place rinsed beans in a large pot with 8 cups of water, onion, 4 garlic cloves, bay leaf, 2 árbol chiles, and 3 tablespoons olive oil over medium heat. Once water is boiling, cover pot with lid and lower heat to a simmer.

4. Cook for 2 hours, then add 3 1/2 cups of water and continue cooking for another 2 hours on a simmering heat with the lid on the pot.

5. Once beans are fork-tender, add salt and mix to combine.

6. Remove and discard onion, bay leaf, and arbol chiles. Drain beans but reserve cooking liquid.

7. Heat 3 tablespoons olive oil in a large frying pan over low heat.

8. Smash 4 garlic cloves.

9. Fry 2 árbol chiles and smashed garlic until browned and fragrant, about 2 minutes on each side, then remove from oil.

10. Add drained beans to oil and turn the heat up to medium. Mix beans with oil to combine and bring to a boil.

11. Use a potato masher to mash beans until smooth. If beans are a bit dry, add 1/4 to 1/2 cup cooking liquid and mix to combine.

PAPAS CON CHORIZO
Chorizo with Potatoes

Makes 3 cups
Preparation time: 20 minutes
Cooking time: 35 minutes

Chorizo con papas *is a base to many dishes. It can be enjoyed as a side dish, scrambled with eggs, topped with a sunny-side-up egg, crumbled on top of* molletes *[see page 80], or used to stuff gorditas, tacos, or breakfast burritos. The options are endless with this fantastic combo! —Nicole*

9 ounces chorizo, soy, beef, or pork

3 tablespoons vegetable oil

3 large potatoes, peeled, cut into 1-inch cubes, boiled for 15 minutes, and drained

1/4 teaspoon salt

1/8 teaspoon pepper

1/2 cup thinly sliced onion

1. Remove chorizo from casing and set aside.

2. Add vegetable oil to a non-stick frying pan over medium high heat. Allow to get hot.

3. Add potato cubes. Season potatoes with salt and pepper and fry on each side for 7 to 10 minutes or until golden crisp.

4. Remove potatoes from pan and set aside.

5. In the same pan, add onions and sauté for 3 minutes.

6. Add chorizo to sautéed onions and break it up with the back of the spatula. Mix to combine. Cook chorizo according to the type you use: 5 minutes for soy, 12 minutes for beef, 15 minutes for pork.

7. Mix potatoes back into the chorizo mixture. Cook for an additional minute and serve warm.

ARROZ CON ELOTE Y CILANTRO
Corn and Cilantro Rice

Serves 6
Preparation time: 20 minutes
Cooking time: 20 minutes

This simple rice is the perfect tasty side to any savory breakfast meal without overpowering—it just adds a layer of flavor. It can be served with a side of refried beans, under a pour of mole, or as a side to pozole.
—Nicole

2 cups extra-long grain rice

4 tablespoons butter or oil

1/2 cup white onion, chopped

1 cup corn kernels, fresh or frozen

3 large cloves of garlic, minced

1 teaspoon salt

1/2 teaspoon black pepper

4 cups broth (vegetable or chicken)

1/2 cup fresh cilantro leaves

1.	Melt butter in a heavy-bottom pot over medium heat. Add rice and mix to coat in the butter. Brown rice for 3 to 4 minutes or until half of mixture is browned.

2.	Add onion and mix into rice. Continue to sauté for 2 to 3 minutes.

3.	Add corn and garlic and continue to sauté for 2 minutes.

4.	Stir in salt and pepper.

5.	Pour in broth and bring to a boil, about 10 minutes.

6.	Add cilantro leaves and mix to combine.

7.	Cover pot with lid, lower heat to a simmer, and cook for 20 minutes.

8.	Remove from heat and allow to sit for 5 minutes before fluffing.

TORTILLAS DE HARINA

Flour Tortillas

Makes 13
Preparation time: 20 minutes
Resting time: 2 hours
Cooking time: 15 minutes

Flour tortillas act as an edible utensil at mealtime. They are used to scoop up food in place of a fork or spoon. They are the perfect vessel for a breakfast burrito. They can be eaten with a meal or simply with a smear of butter. —Nicole

2 3/4 cups all-purpose flour

2 teaspoons salt

1 teaspoon baking powder

6 1/2 tablespoons lard or vegetable shortening, divided

1 cup warm water

1. Sift flour, salt, and baking powder together in a large mixing bowl.

2. Work 6 tablespoons lard or vegetable shortening into the flour mixture using your hands until flour is crumbly, about 4 minutes.

3. Slowly pour in water and mix flour until dough forms a smooth ball.

4. Knead dough in mixing bowl for several minutes until no dough is stuck to the walls of the bowl.

5. Rub 1/2 tablespoon of lard or vegetable shortening between both hands to warm, then smear over the top of the dough to coat.

6. With the dough in the bowl, cover with a kitchen towel and let rest for 2 hours.

7. Warm a *comal* or skillet over medium heat.

8. Divide the dough into 13 equal-sized balls.

9. Using a well-floured rolling pin and on a floured surface, roll each ball of dough into a thin, round disk.

10. Place dough on hot *comal* and cook for 30 to 40 seconds or until brown spots form on white dough. The tortilla may puff; if so, gently press down on it with the back of a spatula.

11. Cook tortilla on other side.

12. When done, store in a cloth and eat warm.

Tip: Once tortillas come to room temperature, store in an airtight bag and store in the fridge up to 5 days. Reheat over an open flame or on a warm *comal*.

PAPAS A LA MEXICANA

Mexican-Style Potatoes

Serves 4
Preparation time: 10 minutes
Cooking time: 25 minutes

Everyone can agree that potatoes make a great breakfast side dish. But when you add chile, tomato, and onion—also known as the Mexican flag (chile, tomate y cebolla)—your dish becomes the perfect spicy side to accompany with creamy refried beans and eggs. Remove the seeds if you prefer a tamer version of this beloved traditional favorite. —Ericka

1/4 cup cooking oil

2 cups potatoes, peeled and chopped

2 cloves of garlic, finely chopped

2 jalapeño chiles, seeds and stem removed, finely chopped

2/3 cup white onion, chopped

3 Roma tomatoes, finely chopped

2/3 cup water

1 teaspoon salt

1 cup cubed Monterey Jack cheese

1 tablespoon fresh cilantro, chopped

1. Heat oil in a large frying pan over medium-high heat.

2. Add potatoes and cook for 10 minutes, stirring frequently or until potatoes cook through and begin to crisp.

3. Add garlic; cook for 3 minutes, stirring frequently.

4. Reduce heat to medium. Add jalapeños and onion; cook until onion is translucent.

5. Add tomatoes, water, and salt. Simmer for 8 minutes, stirring frequently.

6. Turn heat off. Add cheese cubes and cover. Let cheese soften for 5 minutes before serving.

7. Garnish with fresh cilantro.

TORTA DE PAPA CON RAJAS POBLANAS

Poblano Hash Browns

Serves 6
Preparation time: 30 minutes
Cooking time: 25 minutes

Crispy to perfection with just the right amount of spice will keep these poblano hash browns on the menu for many moons to come. This torta de papa con rajas poblanas *is made in a large frying pan and then cut to share family-style. It is most delicious served with egg, flour tortillas, and your choice of meat.*
—Nicole

1 poblano chile	1 teaspoon salt
2 large or 4 small potatoes	1/2 teaspoon black pepper
1/4 teaspoon red chile flakes	1/2 teaspoon garlic powder
1/4 teaspoon oregano	3 tablespoons vegetable oil

1. Place poblano chile over an open flame and char on all sides. [See detailed instructions on page 5.]

2. Place chile in a plastic zip bag and allow to steam in its own heat for 20 minutes.

3. Remove chile from bag and gently scrape with a butter knife until all charred skin is removed.

4. Remove stem and seeds from the inside of chile, then cut into thin strips. Set aside.

5. Peel and grate potatoes.

6. Take grated potatoes and place them in a kitchen towel or cheesecloth and wring out all the liquid.

7. Place the potatoes in a mixing bowl with poblano chile strips, red chile flakes, oregano, salt, pepper, and garlic powder. Mix with your hands to completely combine.

8. Heat vegetable oil in a large frying pan over medium heat. Once oil is hot, place potato mixture in an 8-inch circular form in the pan. Fry until crisp, about 10 to 12 minutes, then flip and fry the other side for 10 to 12 minutes.

9. Remove from pan and drain on a paper towel or paper bag.

10. Cut into six even pieces and serve.

FRIJOLES NEGROS REFRITOS

Refried Black Beans

Serves 4–6
Preparation time: 10 minutes
Cooking time: 15 minutes

Spread them on your molletes, *serve them with your morning eggs, or just scoop them up with a tortilla chip. These refried black beans are so easy to prepare—you can even use canned beans! —*Ericka

1/4 cup cooking oil

1/3 cup finely chopped white onion

4 cups cooked and seasoned black beans, drained

1/4 teaspoon salt, or to taste

Cubed queso fresco for serving

Totopos or tortilla chips for serving

1. Heat oil in a large frying pan over medium heat. Add onion and stir. Cook until onion is tender, about 3 minutes; do not burn.

2. Carefully add black beans; cook for 2 minutes, then smash with bean masher until desired consistency.

3. Reduce heat to medium-low and bring beans to a simmer; add salt if needed. Simmer for 10 minutes or until beans easily lift from pan when stirring.

4. Serve with cubed queso fresco and *totopos*.

MOLE AMARILLO
Yellow Mole

Serves 6–7
Preparation time: 30 minutes
Cooking time: 40 minutes

This yellow mole is very easy to make with just a few ingredients. It can be served over a batch of quick-fried and stuffed tortillas for a plate of enmoladas de pollo *[see page 91] or over rice and vegetables. The finishing touch to this mole is sliced* hierba santa. *If you are unable to find* hierba santa, *mint can always be used as a substitute.* —Nicole

4 Roma tomatoes

4 guajillo chiles, stems removed

1 cup prepared yellow corn masa

6 cups broth (chicken or vegetable)

2 dry árbol chiles, stems removed

1/4 teaspoon ground cloves

1/4 teaspoon cumin

1/2 tablespoon salt

2 leaves Mexican pepperleaf, sliced into 1/4-inch strips

1. Boil tomatoes and guajillo chiles in a pot for 30 minutes or until tender.

2. Set aside guajillo chiles.

3. Place boiled tomatoes in blender and blend on high until smooth.

4. Drain all water and return the pot to medium-high heat.

5. Strain tomato mixture into heated pot by whisking the mixture through a sieve.

6. Bring tomato mixture to a slight boil, then lower the heat to low. After 5 minutes, add 2 cups broth.

7. Into a blender, add yellow corn masa and 2 cups broth; blend on high until smooth.

8. Strain into tomato pot through a sieve.

9. Whisk together until tomato mixture thickens, about 10 minutes.

10. Add rehydrated guajillos chiles and árbol chiles, ground cloves, cumin, salt, and 2 cups broth to a blender and blend on high for 1 minute.

11. Pour chile mixture into tomato mixture through a sieve, whisking the chile mixture while in the sieve to remove any seeds or particles of skin.

12. Rinse whisk, then whisk the mixture in pot for another 10 minutes or until the mole thickens.

13. Add Mexican pepperleaf and continue to simmer for 10 to 15 minutes.

14. Remove from heat and use as desired.

SOMETHING SWEET

SWEET

Algo Dulce

GALLETAS DE AVENA, AMARANTO Y ARÁNDANOS

Amaranth and Oatmeal Breakfast Cookies with Cranberries

Makes 12
Preparation time: 20 minutes
Baking time: 20 minutes
Refrigeration time: 30 minutes
Cooling time: 5 minutes

Cookies for breakfast? Yes, please! These protein-packed cookies will make you feel like you are cheating. Crispy on the outside and soft on the inside, they make a great accompaniment to your morning coffee or milk. Kids will love them too! —Ericka

1/2 cup butter, room temperature

1/2 cup brown sugar, packed

3 tablespoons raw honey

2 eggs

1 teaspoon baking powder

1/4 teaspoon salt

1 cup all-purpose flour

1/2 cup whole oats

1 1/2 cups puffed amaranth, divided

1/2 cup dried cranberries

1. Preheat oven to 350°F.

2. Line a large baking sheet with parchment paper. Set aside.

3. Combine butter and brown sugar in a stand mixer. Mix at medium speed until creamy.

4. Add honey, eggs one at a time, baking powder, salt, and flour 1/4 cup at a time.

5. Reduce mixer speed to low, add oats, 1/2 cup amaranth, and cranberries; continue mixing until all ingredients are mixed well, about 2 minutes.

6. Refrigerate cookie dough in mixing bowl for 30 minutes.

7. Place remaining amaranth in a medium bowl.

8. Scoop out 2 tablespoons cookie dough and roll between palms.

9. Roll each dough ball in amaranth to coat evenly.

10. Arrange coated dough balls 1 1/2–inches apart on prepared baking sheet. Lightly press each ball to form a thick patty.

11. Bake for 15 to 18 minutes or until edges are golden.

12. Cool for 5 minutes on baking sheet, then transfer to cooling rack.

GALLETAS DE PLÁTANO Y ALMENDRAS

Banana Almond Breakfast Cookies

Makes 12–14
Preparation time: 10 minutes
Refrigeration time: 20 minutes
Cooking time: 20 minutes
Cooling time: 10 minutes

We always have a bunch of bananas in our fruit bowl. Occasionally, a couple get forgotten and over-ripen. So, I make these banana almond breakfast cookies to enjoy with milk or coffee, as well as to include in my son's lunchbox. They are gluten-free and made in a short amount of time. —Ericka

2 very ripe bananas

1 cup rolled oats

1 cup almond flour

1/2 cup almond butter

1 tablespoon honey

1/2 cup chocolate chips

1. Preheat oven to 350°F.

2. Line a baking sheet with parchment paper. Set aside.

3. Mash bananas in a large bowl with a fork.

4. Add oats, almond flour, almond butter, honey, and chocolate chips. Stir until ingredients have mixed well.

5. Refrigerate for 20 minutes.

6. Scoop out 2 tablespoons and shape into a ball. Mixture will be sticky.

7. Place on prepared baking sheet and flatten to 1/4 inch.

8. Repeat with remaining mixture.

9. Bake for 15 to 20 minutes or until underside of cookies is golden-brown.

10. Cool on tray for 10 minutes.

ARROZ CON LECHE DE PLÁTANO

Banana Rice Pudding

Serves 6
Preparation time: 20 minutes
Cooking time: 20 minutes

If you like bananas and arroz con leche, *then this is the perfect warm breakfast for you! If you don't like hot* arroz con leche, *don't fret because this banana pudding can be enjoyed hot, cold, or at room temperature. Make plenty! Everyone will enjoy it and ask for seconds and thirds.* —Ericka

1 cup long grain rice

5 cups water, divided

1 cinnamon stick

3 whole cloves

3 cups whole milk

1/2 cup sugar

3 bananas, chopped in small pieces

Ground cinnamon for garnish

1. Soak rice in 2 cups water for 20 minutes and then drain.

2. In a large saucepan, place 3 cups water, cinnamon stick, and cloves over medium heat. Bring to a boil.

3. Add rice and simmer until most of the water has been absorbed and rice is tender but not dry, about 15 minutes.

4. Add milk. Decrease heat to low and stir until mixture begins to simmer.

5. Add sugar and bananas and continue to stir for 5 minutes.

6. Remove from heat and let cool. Mixture will thicken.

7. Serve and garnish with cinnamon.

PANQUÉ DE PLÁTANO AL RON
Banana Rum Loaf

Serves 8
Preparation time: 15 minutes
Baking time: 1 hour 15 minutes
Cooling time: 2 hours

This banana loaf is welcome at any breakfast table. Many people will have a slice of banana bread with a cup of coffee as a quick way to start the day. It is the pre- or post-breakfast sweet for many. It can also be used to make banana rum French toast [see page 140]. I personally enjoy heating it up in the toaster oven and eating it warm with a little bit of butter smeared on top. —Nicole

1 cup brown sugar, packed

1/4 cup vegetable oil

1/3 cup crema mexicana

2 eggs

1 tablespoon rum

1 1/2 cups all-purpose flour

1/2 teaspoon salt

1 1/4 teaspoon baking soda

5 ripe bananas, divided

1 tablespoon sugar

1. Preheat oven to 350°F.

2. Spray an 8.5x4.5 loaf pan with a non-stick baking spray. Line with parchment paper or wax paper; leave an overhang of paper on the longer sides of the pan.

3. Mix brown sugar, vegetable oil, and crema mexicana in a stand mixer with paddle attachment on medium speed for 3 minutes until completely combined.

4. Add eggs and rum and continue mixing for another 2 minutes. Scrape down the sides of the bowl with a rubber spatula.

5. In a separate mixing bowl, sift flour, salt, and baking soda together.

6. Pour dry ingredients into cream/rum mixture. Mix until combined.

7. Add 4 ripe bananas into mixture and mix on medium-high until bananas are broken up and almost completely mashed into the mixture. It is okay if there are little chunks of banana in the mixture; this will give the bread nice pops of banana flavor!

8. Pour batter into prepared loaf pan.

9. Top with 1 banana sliced lengthwise.

10. Sprinkle sugar over the top of the loaf; this will create a nice, sweet crust on top.

11. Bake for 70 to 75 minutes or until toothpick inserted comes out clean.

12. Allow bread to cool in pan for 2 hours before removing and slicing.

CAJETA
Goat Milk Caramel

Serves 12
Preparation time: 5 minutes
Cooking time: 1 hour
Cooling time: 5 hours

Cajeta *is a milk caramel made with goat's milk. It is perfect poured over desserts and can be used to coat your cup of coffee. This Mexican sweet sauce is commonly packaged in little wooden boxes when store-bought and is enjoyed more like candy. —Nicole*

3 cups goat milk

1/2 cup sugar

1 teaspoon vanilla extract

1/4 teaspoon salt

1/4 teaspoon baking soda

1. Add all ingredients to a large heavy-bottom pot over medium heat.

2. Stir mixture occasionally to dissolve sugar; this will take about 12 minutes.

3. Continue mixing for an additional 30 minutes with a wooden spoon. This constant mixing will keep the mixture from scorching. The mixture will darken and thicken.

4. Reduce heat to medium-low.

5. Continue cooking and stirring for an additional 15 minutes until mixture thickens and easily parts for a second when you run your spoon across the bottom of the pot. Remove from heat.

6. Carefully scrape *cajeta* from pot into a glass jar.

7. Allow to cool to room temperature for 5 hours.

8. Cover with lid and refrigerate for up to 2 weeks.

   Tip: The longer you cook the *cajeta*, the more it will thicken. If you reach the consistency desired before the 1-hour mark, feel free to remove from heat.

EMPANADAS DE ATE DE GUAYABA Y QUESO

Guava and Cheese Hand Pies

Makes 12
Preparation time: 40 minutes
Chilling time: Overnight
Baking time: 20 minutes

These empanadas come together in no time once the crust is made. The combination of savory queso fresco and sweet guava paste is a pairing that will withstand the test of time. These lovely, flakey empanadas are a perfect way to start your day with a cup of coffee, or serve them for a fancy brunch with champagne. Your guests will ask if they can pack a couple of empanadas to take home! —Nicole

DOUGH

3 cups all-purpose flour

1/4 cup sugar

1 1/2 teaspoons salt

1/3 cup vegetable shortening, frozen

1 1/4 cups butter, cut into tabs, frozen

1/2 cup ice-cold water

EMPANADAS

12 ounces queso fresco

12 ounces guava paste

1/4 cup + 1/16 teaspoon sugar, divided

1 tablespoon flour

1 egg

1/16 teaspoon salt

Dough

1. Place flour, sugar, and salt into a food processor. Pulse to combine.

2. Add vegetable shortening and pulse until fat is cut into flour.

3. Add butter in three parts, pulsing after each addition. Do not over pulse; you are looking for pea-sized balls of butter to remain.

4. Add cold water 1 tablespoon at a time. Pulse once between each addition.

5. Dump dough onto a clean surface.

6. Run hands under cold water for a few minutes.

7. Dry hands well, then quickly press dough together to form a long log. Divide the log in half and form each half into a disk.

8. Wrap each disk in plastic wrap and place in the fridge overnight.

Empanadas

1. Slice queso fresco and guava paste each into twelve 1/4-inch-thick slices. Set aside.

2. Preheat traditional oven to 425°F or convection oven to 400°F. Line two baking sheets with parchment paper. Set aside.

3. On a floured surface, roll each dough disk into a 14x12-inch rectangle about 1/8-inch thick.

4. Cut each rectangle into six equal parts.

5. Fill each piece of dough with one slice of queso fresco sprinkled with 1 teaspoon sugar and topped with one slice of guava paste.

6. Carefully pull one corner of each dough piece to its opposite corner to enclose the filling and create a half-moon shape.

7. With your finger, press the ends of the dough together, then roll the ends of the dough an inch toward the center, keeping the half-moon shape.

8. Dip the tines of a fork in flour and press on the outer ends of the dough to really enforce the closure.

9. Place six empanadas 2 inches apart on each prepared baking sheet.

10. Prepare egg wash by mixing egg, salt, and 1/16 teaspoon sugar.

11. Brush each empanada with egg wash.

12. Make several little slits on each empanada with a small paring knife to allow ventilation.

13. Bake for 20 minutes or until golden brown on top.

14. Place on cooling rack and allow to come to room temperature before eating.

MERMELADA DE FLOR DE JAMAICA CON MANZANA

Hibiscus and Apple Marmalade

Makes 2 1/2 cups
Preparation time: 10 minutes
Cooking time: 50 minutes
Cooling time: 15 minutes

Hibiscus blooms are not just for agua fresca; you can also use them to make your very own sweet hibiscus marmalade! In just one hour, the combination of hibiscus and green apple will turn into a smooth spread for toast or a peanut butter sandwich. The taste is not only sweet, but it is also that tangy flavor hibiscus is known for. —Ericka

4 cups hibiscus blooms, rinsed

2 small green apples, peeled and grated

1 1/2 cups sugar

2 1/2 cups water

1. Combine all ingredients in a large saucepan over medium heat; stir.
2. Bring to a boil then reduce heat to medium-low.
3. Simmer for 50 minutes, covered, stirring occasionally.
4. Let cool for 15 minutes.
5. Transfer mixture to a blender and blend until smooth. Add a few tablespoons of water if mixture is too thick.
6. Transfer to a jar with a tight seal.
7. Spread on buttered bolillos, toast, or *pan dulce*.

   Note: Marmalade will last up to 10 days in a tightly sealed container and refrigerated.

MAGDELENAS DE HORCHATA Y CEREZAS
Horchata Cherry Muffins

Makes 10
Preparation time: 20 minutes
Baking time: 40 minutes

These wonderful muffins are touched with the perfect balance of cinnamon horchata and pops of fresh cherries for a delightful morning breakfast on the go. Pair with a cup of café de olla *[see page 43] and you have a winning combo. —Nicole*

1 1/2 cups fresh cherries

3 cups flour

3 teaspoons baking powder

1/2 teaspoon salt

1/2 teaspoon ground cinnamon

1/2 cup vegetable oil

1/2 cup butter, room temperature

1 1/4 cups sugar

3 eggs

1/2 teaspoon almond extract

1 cup creamy horchata [see page 35]

1. Preheat oven to 350°F.

2. Line an extra-large muffin tin with baking cups or parchment paper.

3. Wash and pit cherries. Set aside.

4. In a separate bowl, whisk flour, baking powder, salt, and cinnamon together.

5. Remove 1/2 cup flour mixture and sprinkle it over the cherries. Mix with a spoon to make sure the cherries are dusted.

6. Add vegetable oil and butter to a stand mixer. Mix on medium speed until combined.

7. Mix in sugar until completely combined.

8. Add eggs and almond extract. Mix on medium speed until ingredients come together.

9. Mix dry ingredients into butter/egg mixture.

10. Add horchata and mix to combine.

11. Add cherries and mix.

12. Fill each muffin cavity with 1/2 cup batter.

13. Bake for 20 minutes.

14. Rotate pan and bake for an additional 10 minutes.

PAN DE ELOTE
Mexican Corn Bread

Serves 12
Preparation time: 15 minutes
Baking time: 50 minutes
Cooling time: 1 hour

Pan de elote *is a creamy custard-like cake-bread that is super moist, unlike American corn bread. It is made with fresh corn kernels and very little flour for that prevalent corn taste. This delicious treat will gladly join you at your breakfast table to help greet the day.* —Nicole

3 eggs

4 cups fresh corn kernels, divided

1 can (14 ounces) sweetened condensed milk

5 tablespoons salted butter, room temperature

2 1/2 teaspoons baking powder

1/2 cup all-purpose flour

1. Preheat oven to 350°F.

2. Spray a 9x13 baking pan with non-stick baking spray and set aside.

3. Separate egg yolks from whites.

4. Add egg yolks, 3 cups corn, sweetened condensed milk, and butter to a blender and blend on high for 3 minutes or until smooth.

5. Pour smooth corn mixture into a large mixing bowl. With a rubber spatula, mix in remaining cup of corn, baking powder, and flour.

6. Whisk egg whites with a mixer until stiff peaks form, then gently fold into the corn batter.

7. Pour corn batter into prepared baking pan.

8. Bake on middle rack for 50 minutes or until toothpick inserted in the center comes out clean.

9. Allow to cool for 1 hour before slicing.

PANQUÉ DE NUEZ
Pecan Bread Loaf

Serves 6
Preparation time: 15 minutes
Cooking time: 45 minutes
Cooling time: 30 minutes

The breakfast table is not complete without a nice loaf of sweet bread. It's the best way to accompany your morning coffee after a spicy dish. This pecan bread loaf, or panque de nuez, *is soft, spongy, and easily customizable if you prefer to add chocolate chips or dried fruit.* —Ericka

1 1/2 cups granulated sugar

3 eggs, room temperature

3/4 cup vegetable oil

1/4 cup whole milk

1 teaspoon vanilla extract

1 1/2 cups all-purpose flour

1 1/2 teaspoons baking powder

1 cup pecans, chopped, divided

1. Preheat oven to 350°F.

2. Spray an 8.5x5.5 loaf pan with non-stick cooking spray. Set aside.

3. Combine sugar and eggs in a large mixing bowl. Mix with an electric mixer for 5 minutes at high speed or until mixture is creamy.

4. Add oil, milk, and vanilla and mix for 30 seconds at medium speed.

5. Sift together flour and baking powder and fold into mixture. Do not overmix.

6. Place a layer of 1/3 cup pecans on the bottom of prepared loaf pan.

7. Add half the batter, evenly covering the bottom layer of pecans.

8. Add another layer of 1/3 cup chopped pecans over batter.

9. Add remaining batter and top with a third layer of 1/3 cup chopped pecans.

10. Bake for 45 minutes or until toothpick inserted in the center comes out clean.

11. Cool in loaf pan for 30 minutes.

12. To remove from pan, run a small knife around the loaf's edges, then place a platter over the loaf and invert the loaf onto the platter.

GORDITAS DE REQUESÓN
Ricotta Gorditas

Makes 28
Preparation time: 30 minutes
Resting time: 20 minutes
Cooking time: 45 minutes

I bet you can't eat just one of these ricotta gorditas. A combination of a cookie and a flour gordita, these little delights can be enjoyed as is or with butter, cajeta *[see page 190], or hibiscus and apple marmalade [see page 197].* —Ericka

3 cups all-purpose flour, divided
1/2 cup sugar
1 teaspoon baking powder
1/4 teaspoon salt
1/2 cup butter, softened

1 1/2 cups ricotta cheese
1 cup milk, room temperature
Goat milk caramel [see page 190] or *dulce de leche* for
    serving

1. In a large bowl, whisk together 2 1/2 cups flour, sugar, baking powder, and salt.

2. Add butter and squeeze together with dry ingredients by hand to mix well. Mixture should resemble sand.

3. Add ricotta and continue mixing with hands until all ingredients have been combined.

4. Slowly add milk, kneading by hand. Continue kneading until dough is smooth and no longer sticky. Add remaining flour if needed, 1 tablespoon at a time, to knead and smooth out dough.

5. Shape dough into a ball, cover with a clean kitchen towel, and let rest for 20 minutes.

6. Preheat skillet or *comal* over medium-low heat.

7. Dust working area and rolling pin with flour.

8. Roll out dough and cut with a large 2 1/2–inch round cookie cutter.

9. Remove extra dough and work back into the next batch.

10. Repeat as needed until all dough is cut.

11. Place 3 to 4 dough discs on *comal* and cook for 3 to 5 minutes on each side or until golden brown spots appear.

12. Remove from heat and transfer to a basket or plate covered with a clean kitchen towel to keep warm.

13. Repeat with the rest of the dough.

14. Serve with a drizzle of goat milk caramel or *dulce de leche*.

CONCHAS CON CAJETA

Shell-Shaped Sweet Bread with Goat's Milk Caramel

Makes 12
Preparation time: 30 minutes
Resting time: 3 hours
Baking time: 20 minutes
Cooling time: 10 minutes

Conchas con cajeta *is the perfect Mexican breakfast sweet bread combo for days when it's cold out. Pair* this sticky *pan dulce* with your favorite hot beverage for a cozy start to your morning. —Nicole

DOUGH

3 teaspoons active yeast

1/2 teaspoon sugar

1/2 cup warm water

3 3/4 cups bread flour

1/2 cup + 1/8 cup baker's sugar

1/2 teaspoon salt

1/2 cup unsalted butter, room temperature

2 eggs

1 teaspoon vanilla extract

TOPPING

1/2 cup vegetable shortening

1/2 cup confectioners' sugar

1 cup all-purpose flour, plus more if needed

Goat milk caramel [see page 190] or 1 1/2 cups store-bought

Make the dough.

1. In a small bowl, combine yeast, sugar, and warm water to activate yeast. Mix to combine and allow to get frothy. This will take about 10 minutes.

2. In the meantime, add bread flour, baker's sugar, and salt to a stand mixer and whisk together.

3. Change the attachment to a dough hook and add butter. Mix until all the butter is incorporated and forms pea-like shapes with the dough.

4. Add eggs and vanilla and continue mixing until incorporated. The dough will look shaggy and a bit floury still.

5. Add the activated yeast/water mixture; this will bring the dough together perfectly! Mix with dough hook for about 10 minutes on medium. The dough will be soft and pull easily.

6. Prepare a floured surface and grease a large bowl.

7. Remove dough from mixer and place on the floured surface.

8. Knead for a minute or two and shape into a ball.

9. Place dough in the greased bowl and cover with plastic wrap.

10. Let dough double in size for 2 hours in a warm place (80 to 85 degrees).

Make the topping.

1. Add shortening and confectioners' sugar to the stand mixer with the paddle attachment. Mix until combined.

2. Slowly pour in all-purpose flour until completely combined. If the mixture does not come together easily when done, add a tablespoon of flour until it becomes paste-like.

Shape the *conchas*.

1. Once the dough has doubled in size, divide it into twelve even pieces. Weigh them if you have a scale. If not, try and get them as uniform as possible.

2. Grease two baking sheets and your hands.

3. Roll each piece of dough into a ball and flatten slightly between the hands to make a round, thick disk.

4. Rub a little grease on the top of each dough disk.

5. Once all dough is shaped, place in a warm place to double in size. This will take about 1 hour.

Add the topping.

1. Take a tablespoon of topping and, with floured hands, roll into a ball. Make twelve balls total for the *conchas*.

2. Line a tortilla press with floured parchment paper or a clean plastic bag, then place one topping ball in the middle and press down to make a flattened disk.

3. Carefully remove disk from press and place on top of a *concha*.

4. Repeat until all *conchas* are covered.

5. Score the *concha* topping with a small paring knife.

Bake.

1. Preheat oven to 325°F.

2. Bake *conchas* for 20 minutes or until golden on the bottom.

3. Remove from oven and let cool 10 minutes on the baking sheet.

4. Drizzle the top of each *concha* with 2 tablespoons goat milk caramel and serve.

    Tip: Goat milk caramel can be warmed slightly for easy drizzling by placing jar in a small saucepan filled with boiling water to the halfway mark of the jar for 5 minutes.

BARRAS DE PIÑA CON GRAJEA

Sprinkled Pineapple Bars

Makes 16
Preparation time: 1 hour
Chilling time: 3 hours 20 minutes
Baking time: 1 hour

You can enjoy this sprinkled pineapple bar right before breakfast or after for that much-desired sweet taste. A trifecta, these bars have a buttery cookie base, layer of fresh pineapple filling, and topping of rainbow-sprinkled crust. You can cut the squares as small as you'd like to feed breakfast guests or bigger to accompany your morning café. —Nicole

CRUST

3/4 cup butter

6 tablespoons cream cheese

1/2 cup baker's sugar

2 1/2 cups flour

1 egg

1 tablespoon water

3 tablespoons rainbow sprinkles

PINEAPPLE FILLING

6 cups pineapple, cut into 1-inch cubes

8 ounces piloncillo

1/2 cup + 2 tablespoons water

1 cinnamon stick

2 tablespoons cornstarch

1/8 teaspoon salt

COOKIE BOTTOM

3/4 cup sugar

2 cups flour

1 cup butter, cold

1/2 teaspoon cinnamon

5 salted pecans

1/4 teaspoon salt

Crust, Part One

1. Add butter, cream cheese, sugar, and flour to a food processor. Pulse until dough comes together.

2. Divide into two balls, cover with plastic wrap, and place in fridge for 3 hours.

Pineapple Filling

1. In a stock pot over medium heat, add pineapple, piloncillo, 1/2 cup water, and cinnamon stick. Allow piloncillo to melt completely and bring mixture to a boil.

2. Once boiling, mash down pineapple with a potato masher to break it up. This whole process should take 30 minutes.

3. In a separate bowl, mix 2 tablespoons cold water and cornstarch together until cornstarch is completely dissolved and becomes a slurry.

4. Slowly pour cornstarch mixture into pineapple and mix constantly until mixture thickens.

5. Sprinkle in salt and mix to combine.

6. Remove from heat and allow to come to room temperature.

Cookie Bottom

1. Preheat oven to 400°F.

2. Add sugar, flour, butter, cinnamon, pecans, and salt to a food processor. Pulse until dough comes together and pecans are broken up into little pieces.

3. Spray 9x13 baking dish with non-stick baking spray and then line with parchment paper; leave an overhang of paper on the longer sides of the pan.

4. Press dough evenly into the bottom of the baking dish with your fingers until completely leveled.

5. Bake for 20 minutes until just lightly browned/par baked.

6. Remove from oven and allow to cool to room temperature.

Crust, Part Two

1. On a floured surface, roll refrigerated crust out to 9x13.

2. Cut even strips of dough.

3. Create a lattice top by basket weaving or braiding pieces of dough on a piece of parchment paper.

   Tip: Trace size of pan onto a sheet of parchment paper, then create lattice top on the parchment paper to fit to size.

4. Create egg wash by whisking egg and water.

5. Brush dough with egg wash and sprinkle with rainbow sprinkles.

6. Place in the freezer for 20 minutes to firm up for transfer.

7. Lower temperature of oven to 375°F.

Assembly

1. Spread pineapple filling evenly over par-baked cookie crust.

2. Remove crust from freezer/parchment paper.

3. Transfer lattice crust on top of pineapple filling. Press in to fit to size.

4. Bake for 40 minutes.

5. Allow to cool to room temperature, then remove from pan and cut into squares.

GRANOLA EN LA ESTUFA
Stovetop Granola

Makes 4 1/2 cups
Preparation time 10 minutes
Cooking time: 30 minutes

You will never buy granola again after you make a batch of this stovetop version! It is loaded with my favorite nuts, grains, seeds, and dried fruit, but that doesn't mean you have to include them all. Replace with your favorites and make it your own. Don't eat honey? Switch it out with maple syrup and make it a vegan version. I always have a large jar of this anytime treat handy, ready to top my yogurt, smoothies, or ice cream. —Ericka

1/4 cup raw honey

1 tablespoon vanilla extract

1/8 teaspoon salt

2 tablespoons cooking oil

2 cups rolled oats

1/3 cup raw pecans, roughly chopped

1/4 cup raw almonds, roughly chopped

3 tablespoons raw pepitas

2 tablespoons flax seed

1/3 cup shredded unsweetened coconut

1/4 teaspoon ground cinnamon

1/2 cup puffed amaranth

1/3 cup golden raisins

1/4 cup dried cranberries

1. Spray a baking sheet with non-stick cooking spray or coconut oil. Set aside.

2. Whisk together honey, vanilla, and salt in medium bowl. Set aside.

3. Heat oil in large non-stick saucepan over medium-low heat. Add oats, pecans, almonds, pepitas, and flax seeds. Stir continuously with a wooden spoon for 8 minutes.

4. Add coconut and cinnamon. Continue stirring over medium-low heat for 10 minutes.

5. Stir in honey mixture. Mixture will be humid. Continue stirring for 12 minutes or until mixture is golden and less humid.

6. Turn off heat and stir in amaranth, raisins, and cranberries until evenly distributed.

7. Transfer mixture to prepared baking sheet and spread into an even layer to dry and cool.

8. Store in a tightly sealed jar. This granola can last up to 3 weeks.

TOSTADAS DE TUNA ROJA

Red Prickly Pear Tostadas

Makes 25
Preparation time: 50 minutes
Resting time: 30 minutes
Cook time: 50 minutes

Prickly pear tostadas are sweet, cinnamon-spiced, and crispy enough to dip in oat atole [see page 44]. The perfect comfort start to those cold winter mornings. The prickly pear juice is a beautiful magenta that will color your tortillas into a light pink treat. —Ericka

4 red prickly pears, peeled and roughly chopped
1/2 cup water, room temperature
3 cups masa harina
1 cup hot water

1/2 cup sugar
1/2 teaspoon ground cinnamon
Vegetable oil for brushing

1. Place prickly pear pieces and room temperature water in blender. Blend until smooth.

2. Run liquid through a mesh strainer into a container with spout. Liquid should be about 2 cups. Set aside.

3. Combine masa harina and hot water in a large bowl. Stir with a wooden spoon until mixture is cool to the touch.

4. Knead with hands until water has been absorbed. *Masa* will be coarse and dry.

5. Careful so as not to splash, add prickly pear juice, sugar, and cinnamon. Knead with hands until mixture has absorbed all liquid and easily pulls away from your hands and bowl.

   Caution: prickly pear juice may stain hands and clothing.

6. Cover bowl with a dish towel and let rest for 30 minutes.

7. Preheat *comal* over medium-high heat. Lightly brush with vegetable oil, then wipe with paper towel.

8. Knead dough again and make approximately 25 (2-inch) *masa* balls, about 50 grams each. Keep them in the bowl covered with a kitchen towel.

9. Cut a clean plastic zip bag in half. Lay one piece of plastic on the surface of a tortilla press.

10. Place a *masa* ball on the center and cover with the other piece of plastic. Gently flatten to approximately 4 1/2 inches in diameter.

11. Carefully remove plastic from each side of the tortilla and gently lay tortilla on hot *comal*.

12. Cook for 30 seconds or until edges begin to change color slightly. Flip tortilla to other side and cook for 90 seconds.

13. Flip a second time, to the original side. Tap the tortilla gently in the center; this will cause it to puff and cook with steam inside. Cook for 30 seconds.

14. You can place cooked tortillas in a clean folded kitchen towel or *tortillero* to keep warm, or you can place them on a second *comal* or skillet over low heat to continue cooking until crispy.

15. Serve immediately or store in a plastic zip bag in the refrigerator.

Thank you to my family, **Efrain and Joaquin**, for all your encouragement and support. I love you more than words can say.

Mom, *gracias una vez mas!* Thank you once again for your valued advice, tips, and instilling the love of cooking in me *¡Te amo!*

Telma, Aaron, Sophie, and Frida. Thank you for all the love and support. Love you guys!

Celeste, thank you so much for your friendship, words of encouragement, and for being my on-call taste tester.

Dave S. and Dave Z., thank you for the laughs and the love. You guys are the best.

Thank you to the folks at Familius—**Christopher, Ashley, Peg, and Brooke**—for giving me the opportunity to share my recipes once again.

Thank you, **Atelier Maia**, for providing for the beautiful BAJA cookware.

Thank you so much to all the *Nibbles and Feasts* **readers** throughout the years. Thank you for the kind messages and emails encouraging me to share more. Your words have kept me cooking.

—Ericka Sanchez

My Deepest Gratitude . . .

Thank you to my forever-partner, **Mando**, for making life with you the best thing that's ever happened to me. My world goes 'round with you in it, and I am eternally grateful for your fierce devotion to our son and dedicated love you show me daily.

Ahhhh, and thanks for photographing all my recipes for this book—you're the best!

Thank you to my only child, **Max**, for being such a sweet and caring teenager. You make motherhood my treasure and I can't imagine my universe without you in it. Please continue to smile big and keep the curiosity and zest for life in your eyes. I love you more than life.

Thank you to **my mom** for loving me unconditionally and always being by my side. I don't think I'll ever be ready to cut those apron strings, nor do I want to. I love you so much, Mom, and will take care of you for as long as I'm alive.

Thank you to **all my cousins** who cared for me and put up with my non-stop talking and singing when we were kids. I love you all so much!

Thank you to my sister **Serena** for never allowing distance to create a gap in our relationship. <3 I love you, sister.

Thank you to all **MY FRIENDS** for texting me on the daily and being the most awesome *amigas* with your never-ending wisdom and abundance of kindness! Where would I be without you all?

Thank you to **my Familius family**: The real-life Christopher Robbins, Ashley Mireles, Brooke Jorden, and Peg Sandkam! Thank you for welcoming me into your book club. I feel honored to be a part of the Familius library.

Xo,

—Nicole Presley

ABOUT THE AUTHORS

Ericka Sanchez is a recipe developer, food stylist, food photographer, and the creator of the award-winning website *Nibbles and Feasts*. Ericka was born in Torreon Coahuila, Mexico, and immigrated with her family to El Paso, Texas, at eight years old.

Ericka's website revolves around her life as a bicultural Latina living in California and began as a way to catalog recipes and cherished memories in the kitchen with her grandmother, Amelia, and mother, Carmen, in Mexico. Now her recipe development has led her to reconnect with her Mexican roots by developing her own twist on the traditional.

Ericka has a marketing and social media background, having worked in sports marketing, retail property management, and community management for 20 years.

Her website, recipes, food styling, and photography have led her to work with Fortune 500 companies and a feature in the award-winning Allen Media Group's Recipe.TV network. Her and her work has been featured in various online and print magazines such as Oprah Daily, *Parents Latina, Taste of Home, Eating Well, Cosmopolitan for Latinas, Woman's Day, SHAPE,* and *Latina.* She is a regular contributor to the award-winning recipe websites *Yummly, Simply Recipes,* and *Food 52.*

Ericka is the author of two other cookbooks: *Aguas Frescas & Paletas* and Golden Poppy Award nominee *¡Buen Provecho!*

Ericka Lives in Orange County, California with her husband, Efrain; her fourteen-year-old son, Joaquin; and her two dog rescues, Captain and Chopper.

Born and raised in Los Angeles's eastside, Nicole Presley is a Latina culinary enthusiast and recipe developer passionate about her culture and food. She is self-taught and inspired to keep the traditional Mexican desserts of her childhood alive with her recipes. She is also a master of Mexican-American fusion desserts to honor her dual cultures and take your taste buds on a magnificent culinary journey.

Nicole uses her skills that combine cooking and beautiful food art to create accessible recipes for thousands of followers on her social media platforms, known as *Presley's Pantry*. She has been hired by some of the country's most renowned companies as a food stylist and recipe developer, and has landed her some of the most incredible experiences that continue to shape her footprint in the culinary world. In her first book, *¡Viva Desserts!*, Nicole used her personal and professional experiences to create decadent desserts from her East LA kitchen that pay homage to her roots and celebrate all the sweetness life has to offer.

Nicole lives in East Los Angeles with her husband, her thirteen-year-old son, and her two chihuahuas.

ABOUT FAMILIUS

Visit Our Website: www.familius.com

Familius is a global trade publishing company that publishes books and other content to help families be happy. We believe that the family is the fundamental unit of society and that happy families are the foundation of a happy life. We recognize that every family looks different, and we passionately believe in helping all families find greater joy. To that end, we publish books for children and adults that invite families to live the Familius Ten Habits of Happy Family Life: **love together, play together, learn together, work together, talk together, heal together, read together, eat together, give together**, and **laugh together**. Founded in 2012, Familius is located in Sanger, California.

Connect

Facebook: www.facebook.com/familiustalk

Twitter: @familiustalk, @paterfamilius1

Pinterest: www.pinterest.com/familius

Instagram: @familiustalk

The most important work you ever do will be within the walls of your own home.